# The Performing Audience

*Bernard Huijbers*

# The Performing

Six and a Half Essays on

*Second Edition,*

North American Liturgy

# Audience

## Music and Song in Liturgy

*Revised by the Author,*
*with Redmond McGoldrick*

Resources • Cincinnati

*The Performing Audience* was originally published in Dutch as *Door Podium en Zaal Tegelijk*, © 1969 Gooi en Sticht, b.v., Hilversum, the Netherlands, and translated into English by Ray Noll, Thomas Fuechtmann, Dan Onley, Forrest Ingram, and Lawrence McGarrell.

First Edition: September, 1972.

Second Revised Edition: October, 1974.

Printed in the United States of America

# Contents

# Foreword

This book is an extensive revision of an earlier collection of the author's essays and lectures published under the same title in 1972 in a limited edition. The first edition was translated from Dutch, German, and French by Ray Noll, Thomas Fuechtmann, and Dan Onley, with the collaboration of Forrest Ingram and Lawrence McGarrell.

Initial reaction to the book suggested that the work was destined to exercise considerable influence upon the development of church music in America. Hence author and publisher agreed upon the need for a careful revision of the translations for the best possible clarity and readability. Bernard Huijbers worked directly with Redmond McGoldrick on the task of major revision. We are indebted to the translator for his painstaking care in creating a new and excellent text, and to Natalie Waugh of our staff for equally careful work in the final editing and design of this edition.

We are proud of this book, convinced that it will serve well to illuminate what is happening, what has happened, and what must happen in church music today. The author's own musical compositions exemplify and implement the fundamental concepts and principles set forth in this work.

Most writing about the state of church music in America today is in the form of complaints about what is not happening and about what does not seem to exist. There is a dearth of constructive commentary, offered with competency and insight.

Perhaps part of the reason for the vacuum in this particular branch of liturgical literature is the fact that "taste" plays such an important role in the selection, performance, and evaluation of music. We generally agree with the working principle that "good" music enhances faith and Christian worship, and that bad music weakens and destroys them both. To differentiate between "good" and "bad," we tend to rely on personal taste, and we are further hampered by hazy notions about music itself and its history in the Church.

The situation is improving, however. Liturgical music is being recognized as a ministry. There is a growing appreciation within Roman Catholicism of the fact that an effective music program is built upon hard work as well as talent, and that both the work and the talent deserve remuneration. Liturgical music in America, with all its variant forms and styles, is beginning to develop momentum and pride, vitality and solid new traditions.

It is time to cease weeping over the momentary void we felt in our "sacred" music in the earlier years of this new era. Though we have indeed lost much of the "old" repertoire, we have gained much too. We have new musical riches. There are new masters. And there is a new willingness to learn and grow on the part of today's church musicians, be they organists, cantors, directors, or members of choirs or folk groups.

*The Performing Audience* is a gift from an experienced composer and choir director to all church musicians in the English-speaking world. It is a sharing of hopes as well as

of insights. It articulates necessary technicalities about the
fundamentals of liturgical music, and it does so in an engag-
ing and personal manner.

Everyone who is part of the joyful song unto the Lord
is esteemed and challenged in this presentation: the composer . . . the choir . . . the director . . . the musicians . . . the
cantor . . . and most especially the congregation itself, the
performing audience.

North American Liturgy Resources
September, 1974

# *About the Author*

**Bernard Huijbers** is one of the leading composers of contemporary liturgical music in Holland, where he was born in 1922. Approximately 200 songs, psalm-settings, table prayers, responsorial chants, etc., have emerged from his collaboration with Huub Oosterhuis, the well-known Dutch poet, writer, and practicing liturgist. Seventy-five selections from this corpus have been translated into English and are being published by North American Liturgy Resources in both sheet music and congregational booklet form under the series title *Let My People Sing*.

Huijbers, a former Jesuit, studied under Ernest Mulder during his Jesuit course of studies, receiving the State Certificate for Musical Theory in 1951. After his ordination to the priesthood in 1954, he studied at the Amsterdam Conservatory, and received the Certificate for School Music in 1960. He then served as Senior Master of School Music and Choirmaster at St. Ignatius College, Amsterdam, until 1969. Since that time, he has been composer, choir director, and liturgical team member at St. Dominic's parish in Amsterdam, a center whose liturgical experimentation has drawn international attention.

His development as composer and choir director can be traced through a list of his principal musical activities. While studying under Mulder, he directed performances of Palestrina's *Missa Lauda Sion, Brevis,* and *Papae Marcelli* (1946-51). He composed a *Missa Matris Dei* and *Cantus Organi* (1950), virtually a full length symphony, and *Four Marian Anthems* for a four-to-eight-voice male choir (1949-51). During the period of his theological studies, he added a *Te Deum* (1954) and an *Organ Suite* (1955) to his growing list of published works.

After 1956, performances of religious masterpieces by Schütz, Purcell, and Buxtehude led to the first liturgical experiments, culminating in a Dutch language *Passion According to St. John* for liturgical use in 1959.

In 1961 Huijbers was among the founders of the Student Work Group for a Vernacular Liturgy in Amsterdam, which introduced the vernacular to the student community. A year later this group evolved into the independent Foundation for a Vernacular Liturgy, through which Huijbers and Oosterhuis release their joint efforts.

Since 1961 Huijbers has composed a wealth of songs, hymns, psalm-settings, and table prayers, mostly for the Oosterhuis texts. Eleven Dutch record albums of the Huijbers/Oosterhuis material have been released.

In 1966, at Lugano, Huijbers helped to found Universa Laus, an international group for the study of liturgical music. He has delivered a number of papers before that group, several of which have appeared in European publications.

In 1968 he conducted workshops for composers and lectured on "New Dimensions of Sacred Song" at Seattle University (Washington) and Manhattanville College (Purchase, N. Y.). In 1972 he was visiting professor of liturgy at Loyola College, Baltimore, where he helped to form a new liturgical team and student-faculty choir. In 1973 he delivered a paper at the Universa Laus meeting in Leeds, England, on "Community and Community Singing." His views as a composer of liturgical music have been challenging and original. A collection of his talks and lectures has appeared in Dutch. This material has been revised and translated into English, resulting in the current edition of *The Performing Audience*.

Huijbers' work as composer and choir director reflects his many years of close contact with young people, as well as with their elders, in Amsterdam and throughout Europe and America. He has retained his long interest in school music, and in 1965 composed an opera for young people titled *Erik* (after the book by the Dutch writer Godfried Bomans).

In 1974 Huijbers conducted workshops and lectured in Canada, the United States, and Germany. Under the auspices of North American Liturgy Resources, he is currently engaged in introducing his music to groups in the United States and Canada.

*(Right) Bernard Huijbers*

# *Prelude*

*This book is based on –*

- lectures in Essen, Fribourg, Lugano, Pamplona
  for the international group of friends *Universa Laus*
  who, under a Latin name,
  study the vernacular liturgy

- my articles in professional journals (noted within)

- lectures and workshops
  at Seattle University, Manhattanville College, N. Y.,
  Loyola College (Baltimore)

- above all, lectures to my students
  at the Amsterdam Conservatory and the Institute
  for Catholic Church Music, Utrecht

- reflections occasioned by the reactions
  of people at services and in choirs,
  especially the Fons and Igkoor
  at the Dominicuskerk, Amsterdam,

where I have been Choir Director
and Liturgical Team member for several years

- a question to myself:
how can I assist others
to understand the rationale
which underlies my musical composition
and thus, my music?

- liturgical experiments,
carefully planned
and often repeated.


*This book is intended for –*

- my fellow church musicians,
who thought they saw the ideal of their youth
become inaccessible –
that they be not embittered or discouraged
but dare to climb strange paths
to the future

- the young at heart and young in years,
who have again begun to believe
or are looking for their way –
that they may understand more clearly
what they are doing,
and manage the ascent that is song

- the opponents of renewed liturgy,
at times more harsh
the less they understand what to do –
that they may understand
new wine requires new skins

- student musicians,
  because our future lies in their hands —
  that they may not tarry
  before strange gods
  but cut a new path

- and for myself
  no theologian, no liturgist,
  no music historian or ethnomusicologist,
  no music-sociologist or esthetician,
  but a composer, a music theoretician, and school
    music teacher
  who, from experience,
  must pose questions
  to all the specialists
  that they may sing with me
  or make a better song

  since neither the renewal of culture
  nor of music
  nor of liturgy
  is the work of any individual or group,
  but the result of what we all discover
  together.

*Bernard Huijbers*
*Amsterdam, November 1973*

# *Chapter One*

## Liturgical Folk Music
## as the Language of All

From a purely musical standpoint, what liturgical changes are taking place today within the Roman Catholic Church?
Much more is happening, really, than gradually putting aside
a centuries-old cultural treasure and replacing it with new
music written to vernacular texts. What is happening today
is so unique in the history of Western music that it is difficult to find a parallel for it anywhere. It is this:  music is
now being composed to be performed by professionals and
semi-professionals alike, and to be sung by the mass of musically untrained people present – no longer mere listeners.

Music composed *for* and sung *by* 'performers' and
'audience' alike!  This phenomenon is utterly new (discounting accidental exceptions like Elgar's *Pomp and Circumstance,*
with its community singing of 'Land of Hope and Glory').
We can grasp the originality of this phenomenon by compar-
ing it, for example, with Beethoven's Ninth Symphony, which
set a new standard for all subsequent symphonic composition.

That finale, in subject and design, reminds one of a
liturgical celebration.  It treats of the brotherhood of all men.
And the foundation of this brotherhood is a religious one.

All people are brothers because they are all children of the
Father, of God who lives in heaven — as Schiller puts it in
his *Ode to Joy*.  Beethoven chose (or rather, as his sketch-
books show, he painstakingly sought out and constructed)
a folksong-type melody as the symbol of the unity of all
people.  In addition, he introduced a chorus to represent
mankind and to speak in its name.

But Beethoven never gave a moment's thought (nor
really could have) to the idea of letting people in the concert hall sing together with the orchestra and chorus.  Yet,
what could have been more obvious?  His point is precisely
their participation in the great brotherhood of mankind
and in the spirit of the French Revolution, which by violent
means had created the framework promising liberty, equality,
fraternity.

And yet it never occurred to Beethoven to choose the
most obvious artistic form to express his idea, indeed the
only adequate form possible:  the participation of all in the
song par excellence of human unity.  He had carefully sought
out a folksong-type melody echoing everyday life.  He an-
nounces it with a prelude, first a single line for cello and
bass, then gradually adds more instruments.  After that, he
has it sung, first by a soloist, then by the chorus.  It seems
to be a complete antiphonal song.  But he fails to invite the
people to join in; he simply had no idea of such participation.
For he lived and worked several decades before the first liturgical revival, when Dom Guéranger (1805 - 1875) would
restore monastic liturgy at Solesmes and begin to publish
his masterwork, *L'année liturgique* (1841).

In place of audience participation, Beethoven took refuge in a musical 'development' which by its complexities
represents a break and a contrast with the real intent of his
finale.  The contrast is meaningful because it brings his main
intention more sharply into focus.  Beethoven makes the best
of it, to be sure.  But he missed his chance.  He does not get

beyond evoking a vision. He sketches it, paints it, but he never realizes it in people, here and now, in the silent 'audience.'

What Beethoven did not and could not do, what he could neither conceive nor imagine — that is what is taking place in our own time.


## FOLK MUSIC


One characteristic of this completely new liturgical music which must be taken into account is this: the people will almost always join in the singing. In fact, without their participation, the music itself may well suffer. And thus, with the people singing along as one of the voices of the choir, we shall not be able to do the same kind of music as formerly. The voice of the people sounds different from the voice of the choir, because their musical manner of expression is different, as Orff and others have noted.

In the future, liturgical music will have to bear the characteristics of 'folk music' in the full, technical, internationally accepted sense of the German term *Volksmusik*. And it will have to obey the laws of folk music, wherever there are such. But the difficulty is: what is folk music? No two ethnomusicologists are quite agreed on the answer.

The term 'folk music' and the division of music into 'folk' and 'art' music are characteristic of the Western viewpoint. The invention of this nomenclature is not based on a real familiarity with folk music — just the contrary. Prominent thinkers in Western cultural music discovered phenomena which, on the one hand, had to be called 'musical,' but which, at the same time, were so foreign to Western musical development that they had to be described and categorized precisely by their strangeness. A body of music was collected on the sole basis of this negative criterion, that it did not fit into the development of Western art music. One should not be surprised, then, to find, upon closer examination, that this music was a very heterogeneous collection. For it was difficult, if not impossible, to find positive criteria common to all the forms we include under the term 'folk music.'

It is understandable that confusion has arisen about this terminology. Folk music and art music (also, 'people' and 'artist,' 'popular' and 'artistic') are not mutually exclusive concepts, and cannot be defined in logical opposition to each other.

The German expressions for 'ethnomusicology' make a revealing distinction: *Musikalische Volkskunde* deals with the music of the Western *Grundschicht* (i.e., the unlettered people), whereas *Musikalische Völkerkunde* deals with all forms of non-Western musicality, including the professional forms of that music. [1]

## PEOPLE AND POPULAR –
## FOLK MUSIC AND POPULAR MUSIC

The ambiguity of the term 'folk music' lies in the confusion of 'folk' (people) with 'popular,' probably due to the Western feeling of cultural superiority, that is, the feeling that everything non-Western or not part of Western cultural life should be called (indifferently) 'folk' or 'popular.'

In fact, then, the music to be properly distinguished from 'folk music' is not 'art music' but 'elite music.' And, as it happens, the criterion of what constitutes 'elite music' derives from a typically Western bias toward culture in general and music in particular.

As it affects non-Western music, one might describe this mentality as 'musical colonialism.' But I shall not pursue the matter here, lest we wander away from our subject — Church music in the present liturgical renewal. Besides, such musical colonialism is rapidly and happily diminishing, as an older and condescending interest in the music of other peoples gives way to admiration, however tentative.

Regarding Western music, the rise of the terms 'folk art' and 'folk music' revealed an attitude not yet influenced by the genuine spiritual depth of democracy. Here, again, the criterion is a negative one: 'popular' means not belonging to the world of the elite, the initiated, the professional, or even the advanced amateur.

One of the criteria which scholars employ to determine what is, and what is not folk music is this: folk music, properly speaking, has no notation, no fixed written form — the assumption being that notation excludes improvisation, which is an important characteristic of folk music. But this assumption proves to be a false one. Consider the organ concertos of Handel or today's popular music, which is notated but still allows for improvisation. Once again — a negative and biased principle of selection; 'folk' is taken to mean 'unlettered,' 'illiterate.'

Singing by the people, by the congregation — it seems such an obvious idea. It is the heart of the liturgical renewal. *Liturgy (letos*, people + *ergon*, work, activity) is a social activity. There is no liturgy without the activity and, preferably, sung participation of the people. Yet, in the Roman liturgy, this understanding of 'social' scarcely antedates the beginning of this century.

Modeled after the imperial court ceremony, the shape of the Roman liturgy was developed in the rituals for popes and bishops, elaborated in monastic churches, and propagated throughout Europe by monks. Until now, or quite re-

cently, anyone who wished to form an idea of what the
liturgy was, needed only attend a pontifical service in an abbey.

Let us, briefly, make such an excursion. In the forward
east section of the church, at the altar (formerly behind it),
the officiating minister is seated, surrounded by his assistants
and servers. The Community is divided into two long double
rows, ranged along the walls of the 'choir,' their faces turned
toward the middle, toward each other. Halfway between these
double rows, the *cantores*, when their turn to sing arrives, take
up their position, like the cross-bar of a great H, all of them
facing east. Thus positioned, the monastic Community sing
*to* each other. Their arrangement facilitates and expresses
communion, belonging, contact, participation.

Yet their group is enclosed, as is the choir area, by the
choir fence, which forms the fourth side of the rectangle (at
the bottom of the H). And the fence, or *clausura*, is locked,
as is the monks' living quarters, the *claustrum*, the monastery
cloister or enclosure. But those within do not feel impris-
oned; the real prisoner is the world, which is locked out.

Behind the choir fence, then, out in 'the world' are
'the people.' They are permitted to peer through the bars
of the fence, as onlookers, from the chairs or benches which
were brought in for them and ranged one behind the other,
as in a theatre. They, too, face the east. And they form,
as it were, an extension of the fourth side of the choral
rectangle, pushing back and down into the church, even if
they are outside the fence. They look upon each other's
backs. Well, they didn't come to see each other; they came
to see what's going on up front. They do not sing, scarcely
belonging to the cultic community. (One time, while attending an abbey-service, I was expressly requested not to join
in the singing. Even before anyone there had ever heard
me!) They are not addressed. They receive Communion,
dutifully, once a year.

That was the scene, and the Roman liturgy was designed to fit into it. Cathedrals and abbeys were built to
its specifications.

But how did such a liturgy work in ordinary churches,
especially in countryside places? How could it work where
there was neither monk nor canon, nor office chanted in choir?

There, the choir area has been reduced to the 'sanctuary.' Instead of choir-stalls, we find a priedieu for the parish priest. The area reserved for the people is expanded, but
they remain spectators, ranged in benches, row after row.
The parts sung in the monasteries and abbeys by the monks'
choir and the *cantores* are here assigned to a group of specialists for whom it is hard to find a suitable place. They
eventually wind up against the back wall, up near the ceiling,
in the 'choir loft,' carrying their name to that lofty perch.[2]

Thus, in any case, in the Roman liturgy, 'the people'
have been silent, virtually non-existent, except in its earliest
beginnings. And this, note, is the liturgy we are engaged in
renewing! We ask searching questions about its essence and
we research its oldest patterns. We inherit some relics of
congregational singing — responses and acclamations — but
for the most part, we stand empty-handed.

Ecclesiastical 'law' has long prescribed *what* the people
must do in liturgy; I submit that we shall have to design *how*
to do it ourselves. We, the people, the congregation, will have
to learn that for ourselves! Fortunately, for some time, we
have been permitted the vernacular in our liturgy. But, as
a consequence, we have lost the last bit of music that the
oldest traditions provided for congregational singing.

Congregational singing remains absolutely indispensable.
But this is not because we cannot easily dispense with the
fourth side of the rectangle extended ('the people' were, in
fact, largely absent during most of the centuries-old Roman

liturgies).  Nor is it because we should then be lacking one of the prescribed 'necessary elements.'  What must be insisted upon is this:  congregational singing is *not* simply the singing done by the extended 'fourth side,' by the excluded, the spectators, those lumped under 'the people' at the bottom of a list topped by the priest, the assistants, the servers, the *psalmista, cantores*, and/or choir.  No.  Rather, congregational singing must be understood as that singing done by all of these, forming *one choir, enclosed only by the walls of the church*.  And we are expectantly awaiting the tearing down of those walls, too, so that the church is no longer either jailed or jailer, but rather that the whole world may be able to see us, to participate with us, and we with the world; so that all may, in truth, be one.

There will still be need and ample room for the specialists, the *cantores*, the 'choir' in the strict sense — even a place of honor for those so dedicated.  We shall look to them for inspiration, for instruction, for an occasional surprising extra to listen to and enjoy.  But we hope that they will sing with us when the whole congregation sings.  For they belong to the congregation, and so do all who officiate.

## THE IMPORTANCE OF CONGREGATIONAL SINGING

For Catholic services, then, congregational singing — the song of the entire community — is a new and very important idea.  For central to liturgy is participation, and this is both actualized and further stimulated by good congregational singing — so much so that one may almost say that good congregational singing *is* participation.  As voices join to form one great sound, one feels caught up in it, joined to all the others.  Through this collective sound, people penetrate further toward where they hope they will find God.[3]

This stream of sound upon which one almost floats, by which one is urged on and urges others on, is like a conducting agent closing the circuit between participants, between here and there, between now, then, the last moment, between oneself and all mankind and Him whom we believe to be both behind and embedded in our experience. With this one communal voice for wings, we reach beyond and above ourselves and find we are able to believe, hope, thank. We discover meaning in our transient existence.

One who doubts the power of the communal voice issuing forth from many mouths might do well to reflect upon the London 'proms' or upon any crowded football stadium when a mighty song soars over all, forming one voice, energizing, charging up the players, making something happen. These are happenings, indeed, as liturgy is meant to be. [4]

Congregational singing is one of the principal criteria for judging a liturgical celebration. Wherever good and lively singing issues forth from all present, congregational singing almost becomes a kind of liturgy in itself. Good congregational singing assures the participation of all — even though it is possible, at times, to have a good liturgy accompanied by bad congregational singing.

It should be noted that participation in congregational singing is not a matter of stern duty performed; it is a gift, a matter of largesse. When anyone chooses to join in, he is exposing himself to a degree no one can rightly demand of him. Still, a celebration remains incomplete until all present commit themselves by joining in. [5]

## A MUSICO–SOCIOLOGICAL PROBLEM

One common obstacle to good congregational singing is the marked heterogeneity of the congregation, and the

consequent lack of a sense of community (primarily a socio-
logical problem). How can children, teenagers, adolescents,
the elderly, laborers, members of the middle class, students,
friends, and strangers cohere to form a community, a congregation (a musico-sociological problem)? Within most
would-be congregations, all kinds of musical worlds jostle
and clash. How can they come to terms? How are they
to sing to together?

In the first instance, the question confronts the composer and the conductor, and then the choir, for they set
the tone in the liturgical community. But they, too, live
in a world much different from that of 'the people.' How
can they bring unity out of the chaos they behold?

## THE CHURCH MUSICIAN

Let us view the problem as it confronts the classically
educated church musician. And first, let us profile him. As
intimated above, he is part of the problem, too.

Typically, he has been involved with music since his
very early youth, listening, singing (perhaps in a choir), and,
often, learning to play an instrument.[6] Struggling for mas-
tery of technique by playing and listening, he came upon the
masterpieces of Occidental music. He broadens and deepens
this knowledge, reaching into the distant past. He realizes,
gradually, how musical development started with the most
elementary intervals, via the tetrachord, the pentatonic system, the hexachord and the heptatonic system, moving on to
the discovery of polyphony and the harmonic function of the
bass, leading to forms like the motet, the fugue, and the so-
nata. He traces on through chromatics, enharmonics, wid-
ened tonality, polytonality, and atonality, to the avant-garde
of serial, aleatory, concrete, and electronic music. In any
case, as a contemporary man, he is laden with this accumu-

lated 'historical consciousness,' and with a deep sense of responsibility for the future of the tradition.

As a church musician, he is perhaps doubly serious, longing for a music expressing the deepest human and super-human realities. He may well deem the Vienna classics, and everything which suggests the dance, as inappropriate for re-ligious expression.


## POPULAR MUSICAL EXPRESSION

Beyond his own circle, the classically trained church musician who gazes outward beholds two strange creatures: the expert in popular music and the musical layman.

He may view the popular musician as one who exploits the past with a certain shrewdness to achieve a cheap success, thus misdirecting his talent. If he does, in fact, concede a de-gree of talent here, he still deplores its compromise by coquet-ry, commercialism, and artistic betrayal. The chasm here is far deeper than a difference of tastes; it reaches to the depths of the kind of musical responsibility experienced.

And the gap between him and the layman amounts to total musical incomprehension, as I know well from many years of secondary school music training.

The genuine musical layman (distinct from the ad-vanced amateur) must be considered a true musical illiterate. Even when he has a marked musical talent, it remains un-developed. He neither reads nor writes music, knows nothing of bass lines or harmonic structures. He may have a sense of rhythm, but bars are beyond him. Unless it is heard against the basic meter, syncopation escapes him.

His full attention is upon the melody. He treasures its

moments of recognition, stock phrases, and commonplaces. His residual primitive musicality has been diluted with the musical inventions of the past century. He cannot follow most classical music, and so is unimpressed and unconcerned with it, simply missing its rhythm, harmony, and form. Explanations by the expert are unavailing. The layman complains about his rational, technical approach, and does not trust him.

For the layman, classical music means strangeness, dullness, lack of vitality, suited for public mourning, for the British special Third program or its French counterpart, and he hardly ever listens to it. He is often blamed, along with his host of fellow-incompetents, by the expert (perhaps bitterly) for the loss of the original plain-chant rhythm, and that of the Lutheran chorales and Hugenot psalms. The same expert fails to realize, perhaps, to what extent his own views on church music style and, especially, its rhythm have been influenced by the incompetence he decries. Many of the layman's favorite hymns, e.g., *Silent Night, O du fröhliche, Tu scendi dalle stelle, Minuit, Chrétiens,* are the very songs to which the expert strongly objects.

If these two talk music, the layman is embarrassed, hardly daring to say what he thinks about a given piece of music. He insists he is unqualified to judge. If he is asked to sing, his voice fails. But he can sing quite spontaneously, perhaps excellently, in a crowded stadium or cabaret, or in the shower, or when lulling his child to sleep.

The same reticence stands out in churches with 'dry' acoustics, where our layman feels he is singing alone and that everyone can hear him, because the voices do not merge. Congregational singing requires acoustics in which the individual can take refuge. Poor acoustics must be remedied, by electronic amplification if necessary. Just as is done to assist the preacher and other dignitaries!

Amplification can help, but the self-conscious singing layman senses that he is revealing something of his own personality, and in an awkward, inexpert, uneducated way. He knows he is easy prey to the expert listener, there in the unworldly church interior, with its choir and church musicians, its music so different, its atmosphere so alien to the robust, resounding strains he can join in elsewhere.

Their singing reveals how safe the people feel, how much they dare to reveal of themselves. Only in a genuine community of mind and heart will all obstacles be overcome. And, I submit, both the problem and the solution begin with the composer.

## THE COMPOSER'S PROBLEM

We have seen how our composer has been inclined to regard the popular musician, and the layman out there in the pews. Even if he has passed beyond posing the problem as "I have the music, but how do I get them to join in?" he has only begun. First, he realizes that, in fact, he does not have the music. All that music which had inspired him to become a church musician has been virtually struck from his hands. Next, he realizes that the people are going to have to join in the singing without any real rehearsing. Thus, he must start doing music which is attuned to them and to the situation he and they are really in. Roles are reversed — he is now permitted to join in their singing, even as the choir is permitted to lead it.

So the problem becomes this: what kind of music must he compose (or the director select) so that the people can and actually will participate? Which is to say: the problem of congregational singing is, in the first instance, a problem for the composer and the director. And they are least prepared to cope with it. Their colleague in popular music might know what to do. But are church musicians to humiliate themselves to the point of asking him what to do?

'Humiliate' — here is the key, the turning point from which the required change, even conversion, within the church musician can and must begin. One who finds he may need to 'lower' himself discovers that he has raised himself above the other, and that self-glorification is not a good way to discover, to become yourself. He is now open to some important questions: Is there really nothing good in popular music? Is there, conceivably, something alive there which is precisely what is missing to a great extent in classical music — the rhythm moving so easily across the beat, the abundant improvisation? Where but here find so much music played from memory and by ear? Or such a combination, in one person, of vocal and instrumental music, of dance and theatre?

Could the church musician do as well in these many areas, supposing he wanted to? I believe he would profit by close study of how penetratingly popular music can put across a text, in language the whole mixed lot of people can understand and wants to speak. Or will he continue to turn haughtily away from the expert popular musician, and from the musically uneducated?

But suppose his 'conversion' — the church musician is merely on the trail of the solution. For the problem is not simply one of good will and right attitudes. These but enable him to see and face the strictly musical problem, without compromising himself or his artistic conscience.

The problem of composing for participation in congregational singing is a problem of *musical style*. Which musical style can hope to meet such conflicting demands? It must not be simply at odds with the kind of music consumed by the general public, yet it must not offend the musical conscience of the expert, either. Again, it should not sound too old-fashioned to the avant-garde, nor be too avant-garde to the ears of the average layman. It must not be too difficult for the people to join in with almost no rehearsal, yet it must not be so easy as to offer no scope and challenge to the greater musicianship of the choir.


## THE ANSWER: ELEMENTARY MUSIC

Can we hope to find the answer anywhere except before that point in history at which, drawn by divergent musical interests, the various groups first parted company? I submit that the answer lies back there, where people and styles are still united, the point, area, or musical level that Carl Orff has called *elementary music.* Other composers reveal this same direction — Bartók, Mahler, Bruckner, Tschaikovsky, Brahms, Mendelssohn, Schumann, Beethoven, etc. And it is here, perhaps, that we shall discover the positive criteria for what actually constitutes 'folk music.'

What, then, is 'elementary' music? It is that music in which *the musical elements in themselves are sufficient, used in their simplest form and simplest combinations, and not multiplied, varied, or played off against each other.*

Musical elements are the primal constituents used to construct a melody, a harmony, a rhythm, or a form, e.g., the interval, chord, pattern of rhythm, basic form. Elementary music uses a minimum of such elements; it surprises by the marvel of the least interval, by a long or a short note. It exploits a short but powerful musical idea, brought to full development, fathomed for musical possibilities and for expressive value.

Elementary music is a *relative* idea, i.e., what is elementary for one group of people may be understood and

acquired only with difficulty by another. This applies
especially to certain kinds of folk music, e.g., the 7/8 time
found in Greece, the Bulgarian rhythmic units, various scales
and vocal ornamentation, etc.

Indeed, such music can hardly be said to be 'composed.'
Rather, it avails itself of pre-existing elements, e.g., mi-so-la,
do-mi-sol, or of established characteristics like those just men-
tioned — precisely those things which are not 'composed,'
unless 'composition' be understood in its primary sense of
'putting together,' 'arranging,' and 'originality' as 'variations
on a theme.'

The notion 'elementary' extends to timbre, too: a
vast throng sings — how? fully? shyly? It is this quality
to which the composer must learn to listen, and which he
must learn to love — the *distinguishing sound*, for example,
of the voice with which an old man speaks, a dog barks, a
child cries. For if he fails to discover the beauty of these
sounds, the potential of these instruments, perhaps shrill,
off-key, or hoarse, he cannot hope to play with those sounds
in his thoughts, as he must if he is to compose music expressive of the feelings and intentions embodied there, however rawly, even while adhering to his own honest artistic
creed. The directions he inscribes — *All, Choir, etc.* — should
reflect his keen sense of these alternating timbres, so that
changing them would involve a distinct loss of musical quality.

I believe the 'elementary' succeeds in somehow reaching right into the people, respecting their needs of the moment, including their need, at times, to be silent, and then
to resume singing. The composer's prescriptions to *sing*
ought not come off like a call to stern duty, obeyed mechan-
ically. If the text and the rite, e.g., the Sanctus, of themselves call for the congregation to sing, then the music should
be so composed that it invites (or musically speaking, com-
pels) them to join in.

Elementary music is not the same thing as popular music. One distinction: the former is easily performed by ordinary people; the latter they easily listen to. A stadium in the Netherlands roars out "Hij heeft gewonnen de zilver-vloot," [7] a song no one would ever record for listening, yet a perfect refrain and cheer to hail a goal. Or observe a bus-load of happy singing children – they do not sing, as a rule, the records they love to listen to, because such are not generally performable by the musical laity. Likewise, they seldom choose elementary music to listen to. But when they make up their own music, banging away at an old piano or strummin' on an ole banjo, they can go on for hours – as the neighbors may angrily attest. Elementary! Elementary music in action.

Such music is but a starting point, granted. All music started there, then developed. Stravinsky, Bartók, Webern – all are characterized by a return to the musical elements. But the results were far from elementary, so full of devices and complex arrangements were they. And so with elementary church music; it will naturally develop more complex forms, of all kinds – in time. But at present, the important thing is to find a starting point in a totally new liturgico-musical situation. And the musical sensibility which develops within the community from such a starting point has, I believe, a much better chance of being authentic.

## SOME DATA FROM EXPERIENCE [8]

From my own experience as both composer and director, I find three basic requirements in any piece of music which a congregation today may be expected to learn, to sing, and to enjoy singing. But first, a caution: one should not think immediately of hymns, however popular these may be, or have been, traditionally. True, with their regular stanza-patterns, they present the least difficulty. But nonetheless, the hymn has a quite limited use in a well-conceived liturgy, as I shall try to show later (Chapter Two).

The three requirements are:

a) *The form must be elementary*, which means that it must consist of relatively short, easily-grasped fragments, repeated many times. Generally, there is no real practice time allowed for. Hence, one might say that the practice is built into the music. Here are five distinct examples —

a—a—a, b—b—b
a—b, a—b, a—b
a—b—a—b—a
a—b—a—c—a—d—a
a—b—a, b—c—b, c—d—c, b—c—b, a—b—a, etc.

b) *The melodic fragments must be diatonic*, whether modal or not. Not all the notes of the scale need to be used, of course, and the melody may be limited, for example, to a tetrachord, or to a pentatonic pattern. The diatonic nature of a melody must reveal itself in the intervals, and in the relationships between intervals. The most frequent interval should be the second, then the third, fourth, fifth, and sixth, in that order. By way of exception, the seventh and the octave may be used. Viewed on the treble staff, the average pitch (allowing for exceptions) should be between the notes F (first space) and C (third space) or D (fourth line).

The use of well-known melodic turns or formulas, even when it smacks of plagiarism, is a virtue, not a vice. I emphasize this, since it goes so much against the artistic ethos of so many contemporary composers. This, however, does not exclude melodic finds, but their usefulness will depend on how well they cohere with the rest of the music. Non-diatonic elements can also be used, but they belong with the choir or with the instruments, not with the people.

c) *The music must be rhythmical.* This will mean,
often enough, that it should be metrical. But it is surprising how often the musical layman is quite unconscious of
meter. For him, the rhythm of the words is the important
thing — and this may provide a cue for the composer. The
strength and force of word-rhythm is a commonplace in
textbooks on elementary music, in which words are employed to demonstrate patterns of rhythms. Their graphi-
cal representation, complicated or simple, does not tell us
anything about their singability. The ease of singing depends on the ease with which the rhythms can be caught
by the ear and repeated. Arbitrary turns, capricious
phrasing, complex and abrupt variations, so dear to contemporary composers, are altogether mistaken, since they
render the participation of the people impossible.

The composer will have to translate the pastoral and
liturgical necessity for congregational singing into terms of
musical necessity. As said above, he must learn to love the
sound of a singing congregation; and whether he is modern
or not, he must want to learn to write music for such congregations — much like an avant-gardiste writing for a trum-
pet with no valves. That sound, that function will have to
become as indispensable to his compositions as were the
choruses to ancient Greek drama.

But this does not mean that he will settle for second-
rate art. He must learn that there are genuine esthetic
standards of beauty — and always have been — quite different
from those of the concert hall. These have found a place
everywhere, in every age, in all religions and churches, in
all popular art. And that art, often of the first order, has
been based on what is elementary, on repetition, on the
familiar, on received formulas — and it has been practiced
by the non-professional.

If his contemporaries hole up in their several workshops,
so different from his own, and remain oblivious to that differ-

ent drummer, that other esthetic, very well then, the church musician must pass for non-modern in their eyes.[9]  He will have to seek encouragement from other allies, e.g., from those dramatists who explicitly aim to engage the active participation of their public.  He must expect that colleagues who failed to understand Ravel's nine-fold repetition of the double *Bolero* subject will hardly show any respect for formula-techniques.[10]  He will have to overcome the fear of looking non-modern, e.g., by not evading the need for diatonic congregational singing with some strategem like having the people recite texts in different tones.  Such moves solve nothing.  The problem remains:  how make it possible for ordinary people to sing?

## CONCLUSION

It has been a millenium since strictly ritual music has been composed within the Catholic Church.  For these ten centuries, composers, however talented and prolific, have had to work out on the fringes of the liturgical celebration.  In all that time — no prayer has been composed, no preface, no litany (properly speaking), and no psalm tone!

But today's composer is free to do something for which he would be envied by Perotin, Josquin, Palestrina, Monteverdi, Schütz, Bach, Mozart, Bruckner, Caplet, and Kodály: he is free to enter the 'sanctuary,' with a message 'for all the people.' He is no longer confined to the *Ordinarium Missae.*

Certainly, this entails enormous difficulties for him. Yet he works in an atmosphere probably the most ideal in the whole world of music, namely, in one of the very rare meeting places of the expert, the amateur, and the layman, the composer and the performer, the singer and the instrumentalist.  There, music is undivided; it belongs to the entire community, to all the people.

With so unique a task, and in such unique circumstances, perhaps today's church musician is destined to hear a 'message' intended for the world of profane music, too, where many are "groaning in travail, even until now." If so, I suspect such a message will have implications far broader and deeper than what to sing in church, vital as that question surely is.

**Notes – Chapter One**

1. *Die Musik in Geschichte und Gegenwart, Allgemeine Encyclopaedie der Musik* (Bärenreiter Verlag, Kassel-Basel), under "Ethnomusicologie."

2. See pp. 109-110, "choir."

3. This passage is not intended in some merely metaphorical sense. The people lack a name for God until they turn to him in prayer and song. We pray and sing together, and in that act he receives his name. We launch God out in front of ourselves in song; thereafter we believe and we fill in the void from our experience of life. We cannot believe as soloists. This is not just our need for apostles and other witnesses; it is because we are unable to believe even in ourselves without sharing our belief with others.

4. "making something happen" – what, e.g., makes 'Christmas' happen? A medley of things: the special Christmas gospel and (it is hoped) sermon, the dressed up people in a mood of unique annual expectancy, etc. All these things are the concrete reasons why "it's Christmas!" The traditional date, though now indispensable (and quite unhistorical, since we simply don't know when Jesus was born), is secondary.

5. This theme is exquisitely developed by Huub Oosterhuis, many of whose poems, Table Prayers, and *Fifty Psalms* I have set to music, in *At Times I See,* "Something So Small," translated by R. McGoldrick and Ger Groot, published by New Seabury Press, New York, 1974. A collection of our joint efforts, titled *Let My People Sing: A Series of Songs and Biblical Hymns for Congregation and Choir*, People's Edition, Vol. I, has been published by North American Liturgy Resources, Cincinnati, Ohio, in 1974. Scores for selections in the series are being published separately in sheet music form.

6. See pp. 96-97.

7. a 19th century 'composed' folk song –

|        |        |          |          |          |        |           |         |          |
|--------|--------|----------|----------|----------|--------|-----------|---------|----------|
| *do-*  | *do-*  | *do* /   | *do-*    | *la-*    | *re* / | *do-*     | *si* /  | *do-*    |
| *Hij*  | *heeft*| *ge –*   | *won–nen*|          | *de*   | *zil –*   | *ver –* | *vloot.* |
| He     | has    | cap –    | tured    |          | the    | sil –     | ver     | fleet.   |

8. Compare pp. 37-42.

9. Compare pp. 81-83.

10. See pp. 93, ff.

# Chapter Two

## Limits and Possibilities
## of the Song Form in the Liturgy

*Translator's note:* 'Song' in this chapter translates the Dutch (and German) *lied*, a song in stanzaic form. In other usage, it also includes non-stanzaic forms. The English term 'hymn' designates a *lied sung in church.*

When we speak of folk singing in the vernacular, we usually think spontaneously of the 'folk song.' At first glance, there seems to be hardly any other form. No wonder. As we shall see, forms other than the stanzaic require the support of a larger context into which they are assumed. But this larger context has rarely, if ever, existed, at least so far as folk singing is concerned. The Church, almost alone, might have provided such a context. But it was precisely there that people had to hold their tongues — for centuries.

Thus, many forms, for lack of larger context, were lost to folk singing, leaving only that autonomous form: the stanzaic song, the 'folk song.'[1]

But today the larger context we call Liturgy does, indeed, call for other forms. The present chapter will treat aspects of the song-form in liturgy:

I.   *The form of the song.* The genre 'song' is, indeed, determined by its form. By close observation and reflection, I shall describe this form. Since the 'song form' of composition theory (form theory) embraces more than a single genre,[2] I shall specify the genre to which I refer.

II.  *The liturgical usefulness of the song.* From such a description, we shall be able to assess the usefulness of the hymn in the liturgy. The liturgy itself will teach us that, besides the hymn, there are other musical forms possible, even demanded, at various moments in the rite.[3] We will have to learn that the **function** of singing within the entire context determines the **kind** of singing. It will then be evident that the usefulness of the church hymn in the liturgy is limited.

III. *The possibilities of the song.* Finally, I would ask how within these limitations can the song form be made as good, as useful and adaptable as possible in liturgy?

## I. WHAT MAKES A SONG A SONG?

It is evident that what makes a song a song is its strophic or stanzaic form. But this statement entails a two-fold question of structure:

A. the structure of the strophic song as a whole
B. the structure of the strophe or stanza itself.

## A. The Structure of the Strophic Song as a Whole

A song[4] consists of stanzas, sometimes accompanied by a refrain. The music of the stanzas remains the same; the text changes in content but not in form.

1. Regarding this music, repeated in each stanza —

   a. It is a well defined whole, with a clear beginning and end.

   b. It is so highly concentrated, substantial, and laden with meaning that one singing does not exhaust it.

   c. The number of repetitions within the complete song depends, obviously, on the number of stanzas in the text, supposing all of them are sung; but, conversely, the length of the text must regard the question: how often can people repeat the same music, or listen to it, without becoming bored?

2. The content of the text changes, the melody does not, from which it follows:

   a. The changing word-content must be laden with meaning, constantly say more, in order to render the repetition of form and music acceptable.

   b. The music must be as modest as it can be, lest it divert the singers' attention from the constantly new word-content of the song.

   c. The music should be neutral, so far as possible, or, at least, capable of many interpretations, in order to sustain the changing word content.

3. The repetition of the music and stanza form, while
the word-content keeps changing, has these effects:

a. a certain tension between the two, which
holds the artistic attention;

b. a climax, arising from some magic wrought
by repetition and lending itself to the text;

c. a quality of newness in the repeating music,
imparted to it by the changing text;

d. a unity of contrasting elements, alive in
the interplay of repetition and change.

4. These characteristics combine to produce a closed,
fairly self-sufficient entity — the song, with its own
life and rules, derived primarily not from the context in which it is sung but from the song itself.

In fact, the song determines two special characteristics
of the context of its performance:  it is meant for group
singing, and its repetition of stanzas is comparable to the
repetitions required in folk music.

The song maintains a noticeable balance between text
and music, assigning them, invariably, a nearly equal weight.
Is the musical form determined by the stanzaic pattern of
the text, or is the latter tailored to the stanzaic form of the
music?  It is difficult to say.  As in good poetry (and the
song-text should always be such), one cannot assign primacy
to content over form.

This leads us to the second part of the question of
structure, but I would make this preliminary observation.
When people sing, they usually concentrate too little on
the text and allow the music to absorb their attention.
Anticipating somewhat the analysis of the structure of
the strophe itself, I think this an important phenomenon.

Compare the song with the antiphon (of the Magnificat, for example). The antiphon depends for its whole existence upon the psalm or canticle to which it belongs, and its music is directed towards the totality it serves to introduce and conclude. But a song, whether hymn or ballad, has a closed character, is self-contained. Notice that it can be played, on the flute, violin, or organ, unlike 'open' forms, like the antiphon, the psalmtone, the recitative. [5]

## B. The Structure of the Strophe or Stanza Itself

I shall treat the structure of the stanza only briefly; detailed treatment would contribute little regarding its usefulness in the liturgy. My remarks will parallel those made above about the song — that stanzaic whole of which the stanzas are the parts.

1. The stanzas are nearly always the same in structure.

2. The stanza is musically recognizable as an independent unit because:

   a. it is repeated in its entirety;

   b. with or without refrain, it leads to a 'final' or 'tonic.'

3. The stanza consists of a number of verse-lines, and a corresponding number of musical phrases, seldom fewer than three.

4. The verse-lines are tight-knit by:

   a. a proportional number of feet and a corresponding musical length,

b. related or identical rhythms,

c. a relationship of their last notes such that, in the last line, or in the refrain, the 'final' or 'tonic' is reached,

d. such a turn of meaning and sound as to produce a sense of completion,

e. often, assonance and rhyme, strengthening the structure.

5. The structure, briefly, is not determined by either the text or the music, taken alone, but by their interplay. Granted, each must follow its own laws, without infringement. But this is exactly the point at which mutual influence and penetration begin, such that we cannot really assign primacy to one.

6. Although the stanzaic form must surely serve the content of the text, yet it retains an autonomous life, independent of the situation in which it is performed (e.g., liturgy).

## II. THE LITURGICAL USEFULNESS OF THE SONG

This analysis of the song, the whole and its parts, has revealed it to be a closed, autonomous form, not defined or determined by the context or situation in which it is sung. In consequence, the song has but limited usefulness in the liturgy.[6] Why? Because the liturgy prefers heteronomous forms (that is, forms motivated and primarily determined by the total liturgical service[7]) to autonomous ones. That the Roman Mass liturgy included no songs, strictly speaking, except the five Sequences, is instructive, now that we use them so freely in the vernacular liturgy. They can, indeed, be admitted as exceptions, quite desirable exceptions, but not randomly or as mere fillers. I offer the following indications of their appropriate use.

1. A song can serve to counter-balance the preponderantly open forms in the rest of the liturgy, serving very well, at times, as a rest point, e.g., in place of the Creed, after the Gospel. In the Office sung in choir, a hymn after the psalms and readings serves in this manner. We might note that the Sequence functioned precisely this way; but regarded as part of the entire rite, it was not truly well placed. Coming in the middle of the Service of the Word, it tended to interrupt the flow of the service itself.

2. A song can function well at the opening of a service. If the opening be considered merely as the entrance of the priest, then the song functions merely as accompaniment, and should not extend beyond his entering. But if one attends to the congregation, the entrance song becomes their opening song, setting the tone, laying the foundation for the service. The song can be used particularly well for this purpose.

3. At times, the general movement of a liturgical service may properly be arrested for moments of reflection, of theological recapitulation. Such brief intervals have a closed, autonomous character, and can serve a real need in the service. A song can, at times, serve this need very well.

We have examples of this in the hymns in the Divine Office, after the psalms and readings. Also, in the hymn after the Gospel homily or a Service of the Word, where it serves to sum up and interpret the proclamation. So used, a song can promote active participation.

4. A special instance of the above uses of the song occurs when an autonomous event is to take place during the liturgy, e.g., a wedding, an ordination, a baptism, Songs may both precede and follow, preparing and commenting.

5. A song may be appropriate not merely because of the structure of a particular liturgy, but because of the special circumstances in which a liturgy is taking place. With its closed form, the song is easily grasped in its entirety, and so is particularly suited to occasions when folk singing is envisioned.[8] It can be helpful whenever special care is needed — when the people cannot yet fully participate in the singing or have a quite limited repertoire, or are as yet unable to grasp and feel the liturgical action itself, or lack a choir to help them.

Here I would note the possible usefulness of general songs for the opening, the communion, and the closing. The autonomous character of the song form, in which text and music form a closed unity,[9] makes its use rather independent of the specific day, readings, or performers. Songs can be used for a great variety of occasions, and be used, too, in a variety of ways; there is no law requiring that all present sing each stanza![10]

Finally, an animadversion on translations of the psalms. Some of them were written in stanzaic form in the original and were often, quite naturally, translated in that form. But I would deem it a pity, and a lost opportunity, to render the others in such form,[11] as was done in the rhyming translations of the Reformed Church. That group had reason, since they generally had no choir available. But a well-structured community, with diversified functions, should, I believe, definitely prefer the responsorial or antiphonal psalmody.

## III. POSSIBILITIES OF THE SONG

### A. Form

The liturgical uses of the closed song (hymn) can be broadened by appropriating certain features of the open forms.

1. The verses can be sung alternately, by distinct sections of the group, perhaps all joining in for the concluding verse, as in the Sequences and the hymns in the Office. This can be particularly effective if the text is designed with such alternation in mind.

2. The refrain form is particularly recommended, because it is easily sung by the people, and because it allows them to react, to reply. [12]

Although it is unnecessary to offer schemes of normal refrain forms here, I would note that the use of the refrain as an interjection offers special possibilities, e.g.:

$$a-R - a-R - b-b - a-R$$

It reminds one of a litany. The verse may also be thought of as an interjection, especially if the refrain is long:

$$R - v. 1 - R - v. 2 - R - v. 3 - R$$

Also, to supply a refrain for the verse form, one might have the people repeat the last line:

$$ab \ ab + b, \ cd \ cd + d$$

A striking variant much favored by the poet is the almost literal repetition of the first line:

$$aa \ bb + a', \ cc \ dd + c'$$

## B. Text

1. The text should be biblical in character, and perhaps
   in language, too. For the proclamation of God revealing is inextricably interwoven with history, and
   thus with Scripture. By 'biblical' I do not mean
   the use of Bible texts as a vehicle for the expression
   of one's own thoughts, often quite out of context.
   I mean, rather, a careful search for, and intelligible
   rendering of the meaning-for-us of any given portion of the Bible, always consistent with that book's
   basic themes and intentions.

   The song-text is biblical, as I mean the term, if it
   sets our feet upon the way, especially if Jesus himself opens that way through its words, enabling us
   to read the deeper meaning of the commonplace,
   the seeming trivia and pointlessness, the chaos and
   tragedy of our daily world.

2. The text should be (what other word?) human.
   Teilhard, G. Baum and others have rightly caut-
   ioned on the slippery nature of the concept
   'nature,' especially of the heretofore supposed
   species 'human.' Whatever we are, we are, indeed,
   'unfinished business'! I do not escape this problem, on the level of music, by invoking the notion
   'elementary,' I quite realize. At any rate, a human
   text eschews abstract theological notions and ab-
   hors the mindless repetition of tired, numbing
   credal formulas. It moves with the directness and
   simplicity of the words of a prophet. I fear I
   must say it:  it is elementary.

3. Thus, the language of the text must not be that
   of melodrama, over-blown; nor 'vertical' (quickly
   vanishing upwards). It must mediate *meanings*
   which are themselves direct, simple, and elemen-

tary, yet imaginative and evocative, but in a way always touched with the reserve and respect which, I believe, distinguish every truly human/ religious context.[13]

The rediscovery, the creation of such a language is undoubtedly a task for the poets, of course, and the time for seeking their services is long past due. They have been excluded from liturgy so long, I fear that most of them have lost the language we need, even as so many of us have lost the very sense of our need for that language. Still, my own collaboration as composer with the Dutch poet, Huub Oosterhuis, has provided me an extraordinary proof that the problem can, in fact, be solved.[14]

4. When one of the Readings has recounted some or other *event* (as so often in the Gospel), the song-text can at times re-present it, as a ballad, quite effectively. All in direct discourse, the congregation can recreate it; in the refrain, a section of the group can express the reaction of the ancient 'bystanders,' rendering it present and alive.

5. The function of a text within the liturgy will not be performed automatically by using words that refer literally to that function. An entrance song does not work merely because it employs "go unto the altar" or alludes to something 'beginning.' It would do better to introduce what is to follow, e.g., the initiation of a new liturgical season, or a special celebration anticipated, like a particular feast, a wedding, a baptism. Similarly, the Communion hymn should not belabor "receiving Jesus," or "guest of my soul," etc. It should recreate the background of the event, evoke that event here and now, in this world and in these people ranged here 'horizontally.' Thus,

it should stress "meal," "bread," "giving," "bonds of unity," "death and life," etc.

6. The text may take the form of a dialogue, as between people and choir, man and God. Roles can be changed, with sometimes piercing effect. In this way, mere meditative or lyrical singing by a collection of individuals gives way to a sense of *doing* by singing — and this just where the congregation, as such, has its only chance to achieve community by real participation: in congregational singing. It happens here, if at all.

## C. Melody

1. Community participation in singing can be helped by adapting new texts to old melodies. But one should avoid using those melodies so tied by feeling to their original texts that the coloration will scarcely yield to any other wording.

2. At times, in creating a new song (text and melody), I believe that the melody should be done first. This can challenge the poet, indeed, by a creative discipline, save him from too easy, flat verse forms, even as it can save the composer from the false accents he may yield to, musically, if he must invariably play second fiddle.

3. In their collaboration, the composer and the poet may find the following procedure helpful when the song is to have a refrain. The poet writes the words of the refrain, then the composer sets it to music, *going on* to develop a melody from the refrain music. Working from this melody, the poet now can complete his poem.

4. The melody must be simple but not simplistic. It must have its own characteristic intervals and rhythms. The desired simplicity of a melody is not a matter of "it looks simple" (on paper), nor of notes of equal length, nor of constant repetition of the same tones.

5. The *melos*[15] must be distinctly elementary: not too much based on harmony, nor abounding with a variety of intervals, but rather sparse, not serial or dodecaphonic. If the melody must be modal, then consider a mode not so much a scale with a tonic, dominant, and mediant, but rather the fact that it is determined by typical tone patterns.[16]

6. Close attention should be given to just how the concluding notes of the lines relate to each other, and to the continuity in melody and rhythm implied by these notes.

7. A folk melody should sound good even apart from its accompaniment, a point I would hope can be agreed upon, however unlikely Western musicians are to conceive of a melody which does not imply an accompaniment, and however much a good accompaniment 'adds.'

8. The melody, heard unaccompanied, will generally call for either an arc or a wave construction. In modal terms, an authentic mode will demand an arc form; a plagal mode will demand a wave form. Thus, a good melody seldom ends on a high note, because, taken by itself, the melody has scarcely any other means of cadencing than returning – in the arc form, to the low point; in the wave form, to the middle point. The feeling of coming to an end should arise not only from the added harmonization; the melody itself should evoke it.

9. Something similar may also apply to modulation: while one can hardly object to it in folk song (and Gregorian has related elements), the modulation should really be completed by the melody itself, not leaving the job entirely to the accompaniment.

10. Granted its marked autonomous character, still, the song should be chosen to suit its place in the service, so far as possible. This has been the traditional motive for a Communion hymn somewhat 'lighter' than the Introit. If the closing hymn has any marked character, it should be on the relatively more solemn side. I would note that cantors can be used very effectively in the opening and the Communion song, less so to conclude.

### D. Rhythm

1. Gregorian music, and modern classical and popular, should have taught us, at last, that the word accents and the beats of the meter do *not* necessarily have to coincide. This fact permits the composer to lessen the heavy effect of a text he finds already too emphatically metrical or given to an excessive number of metrical changes. Just omitting the bar lines in the notation helps but little. The song leader/ conductor will still have to determine where he wants the beats; but, I repeat, he is not bound by the word accents.

2. A close analysis of the rhythm of the text itself may yield some striking musical finds. It could even end the long, intractable addiction of 'Church' style to equal note values — which turned Gregorian into plain chant, forced the German chorales into 4/4 time, and debilitated the free rhythm of the Hugenot Psalms. A costly habit!

## SUMMARY

Compared with recitative and psalmody, the song (hymn) is a closed, autonomous form, not defined or determined by its place or function within the rite or service. Hence, it is of lesser usefulness in the liturgy — a caution when we are tempted to make songs and hymns the basis for congregational participation in the vernacular liturgy.

Yet there are moments and situations in which a song can be of service, especially because it adapts so well to those performers for whom it should be intended: the people. It is theirs, they have kept it alive for centuries, by way of folk music, even while they were losing the recitative, the acclamation, and similar forms.

But if the song is to be used in liturgy, it should incorporate some of the helpful characteristics of the open form, and be perfected within the possibilities of its own formal limits.

**Notes — Chapter Two**

1. Compare pp. 47-49.

2. See p. 97.

3. See p. 100, f.

4. Note other meanings of the English 'song': *poetical composition* and *a poem easily set to music*. Also, we are concerned here with the "folk song," not with the so-called "art song."

5. See p. 100, f.

6. The liturgy is a whole whose meaning exceeds that of the sum of its parts; it is much more than the interpretation of a series of texts plus some songs. Cf. Huub Oosterhuis, *Prayers, Poems, and Songs*, pp. 97-118, "The Tent of Meeting" (Herder and Herder, New York, 1970).

7. See p. 100, f.

8. See pp. 48, 64.

9. This is also true of "contrafacts."

10. See below, III. A. 1.

11. Compare p. 98.

12. Compare p. 40, no. 6.

13. See pp. 120, ff.

14. Compare pp. 140, ff.

15. *melos:* not 'melody' but the interval-structure of the melody, prescinding from the rhythm, etc.

16. See pp. 93-95.

*(Right) This song, music by Bernard Huijbers, text by Huub Oosterhuis, was originally composed for use after the homily. It is appropriate for themes of interior conversion, peace, mutual forbearance, etc.*

# People of God

Text: H. Oosterhuis
Translation: F. Ingram
Revision: R. McGoldrick
Music: B. Huijbers

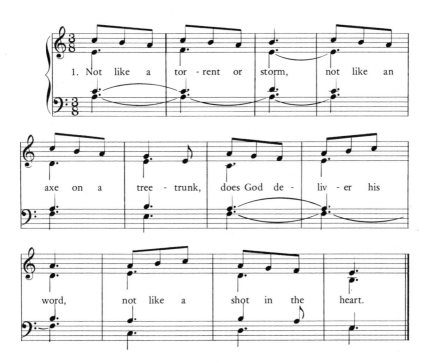

1. Not like a tor-rent or storm, not like an axe on a tree-trunk, does God de-liv-er his word, not like a shot in the heart.

2. But like a gleam of the sun,
   like a green twig in the winter
   peeping above the hard ground —
   such is the kingdom of God.

3. Word that seeks only to serve,
   voice that does not break the silence,
   name that does not open doors,
   stranger of unknown descent.

4. Men melted down into peace,
   children and those poor in spirit —
   these hear his name in their hearts,
   they bear his word in their flesh.

5. Blind men know him by his hand,
   deaf men are able to hear him —
   happy the man who believes,
   happy the tree at the spring.

6. Not in the tomb of the past,
   nor in the temple of day-dreams —
   here he is right in our midst,
   here in the shadow of hope.

7. Here in our dying each day
   we learn that we can believe him;
   we become people of God —
   love now decides life and death.

# Chapter Three

## Latin Liturgy
## and Distorted Development
## in Western Music

### I. PREVIEW OF THE ARGUMENT

In the course of history, the Roman liturgy, and particularly the prescribed use of Latin, have rendered the full
participation of the people by means of singing impossible.
This simple fact has affected not only the people's musical
mentality but also the composition of 'art music.'

For the only way the people themselves might have
had any part in the development of a higher musical culture was, in fact, through their sung participation in liturgy.
Only there did all levels of society and culture — rich and
poor, gifted and ordinary — congregate together, and there
they might have celebrated their community, thus building
it. A common hymnal in their hands and one music rising
up from them, a music composers would have written for
all of them to sing, thus learning to compose for the people[1]
— here is where 'high' and 'low' musicality might have contributed to each other.

But the people had to remain silent, except for a few
scraps tossed to them on occasion. Their folk musicians,

beyond the pale *(histriones, joculatores)*, were in disfavor
here, unlike the wandering bards and minstrels of the ancient Celts and Germans.

And so the composers composed for a select professional or semi-professional group, e.g., the monks, who at
best represented the participation of 'the faithful,' rather
than leading and helping them to participate, and generally
paid no attention to their taste.

Thus, a popular musical language had little chance
to develop, either inside or outside of the Church — the
composers being otherwise engaged. This obtained both
for the early Christian centuries and even after the separ-
ation of sacred and profane music (17th century). For the
latter, insofar as it contributed to musical development,
remained almost as aristocratic as sacred music, once more
excluding the people's potential participation in musical
culture itself.

The only form of folk music which managed to really
prosper was the folk song, the most autonomous and resis-
tant form. Even this prospered only until 1600 in the heart
of Europe; after that, only on the periphery of Western (i.e.,
Latin rite) culture — Scotland and Wales, Ireland, Spain, the
south of Italy, the Balkans, eastern Europe, and Scandinavia.
Elsewhere in Europe, it held firm only in the villages and
the mountain districts, and among fishermen, farmers, sol-
diers, seamen, and tradesmen. The folk song rapidly declined to a pygmy existence, autonomous but isolated, a
miniaturized entity, where it did not petrify into folklore.[2]

Meanwhile, the music of the upper class became the
art of certain performers whose listening audience were
musically inert. With the exception of an odd emperor or
two, this cultured audience neither sang nor played. This
new 'public' merely listened, and perhaps in compensation,
demanded ever stronger concentrations and doses of music.
They directed their attention, first of all, toward the musi-

cians and, later on, to the composers. Improvisation yielded to the written score.

This led to the loss of those instrumental and vocal techniques so characteristic of folk music, e.g., in the Balkans, the near East, in parts of Spain and Italy. Rhythm was simplified to fit the norms of written music. Vocal and rhythmic poverty was compensated for by harmony. There arose a need for the spectacular, for virtuosity, for surprise, for musical separatism.

No surprise, then, that elementary music is now completely abandoned in favor of every kind of theoretically conceivable and professionally performable musical experiment, without regard to the people's taste or level of understanding, not to mention their ability to perform it.

## II. STATEMENT OF THE PROBLEM

As background, here are three quotations from the documents of the Second Vatican Council:

> From the customs and traditions of their people, from their wisdom and from their learning, from their arts and sciences, [the young] Churches borrow all those things which can contribute to the glory of their Creator. . . . . *(On the Missions, no. 25)*

> Even in the Liturgy, the Church has no wish to impose a rigid uniformity in matters which do not involve the faith or the good of the whole community. Rather, she respects and fosters the spiritual adornments and gifts of the various races and peoples. Anything in their way of life that is not indissolubly bound up with superstition and error, she studies with sympathy and, if possible, preserves intact. Sometimes, in fact, she admits

> such things into Liturgy itself, as long
> as they harmonize with its true and au-
> thentic spirit. *(On the Sacred Liturgy,*
> *no. 37)*

(I cannot forgo the comment, anent this second quote:  a
'wish' any honest reading of history attests fulfilled more
in the breach than in the observance!)

> Adapting sacred music for those regions
> which possess a musical tradition of their
> own, especially mission lands, will require
> a very specialized preparation by the experts.
> It will be a question of how to harmonize
> the sense of the sacred with the spirit, tra-
> ditions, and characteristic expressions proper
> to these peoples.  Those who work in this
> field should have a sufficient knowledge
> both of the liturgy and the musical tradi-
> tion of the Church, and of the language,
> popular chants, and other characteristic
> expressions of the people for whose ben-
> efit they are working. *(Musicam Sacram,*
> *no. 61)*

What I would notice about these fine statements, ex-
panding my impatient interjection above, is this:  they all
bear the stamp of 'post-colonial' Church policy and, more
sadly, practice, too.  From the earliest Christianization of
Europe to the Council of Trent, inclusive, such statements
would have been unthinkable.

Specifically, regarding the final quotation, I would
note about "regions which possess a musical tradition of
their own":  are there regions which do not?  And about
the emphasis "especially mission lands":  is it implied
that the peoples of Europe, where the Latin Rite has
always held sway, lack musical traditions of their own?
And if they do, how come?  Or is the implication, perhaps, simply that they have no *folk* music?  And if they
do not, again I ask, how come?

This raises other questions which are not mere speculation but can illuminate the nature of the problem today, and thus help us find our way into the future.

How would Western music sound today if the Latin Church had, in fact, respected the music of the Germanic tribesmen who overran Europe (little of it survives), so anxious (at least, their leaders were) to adopt the music of the civilized peoples they had conquered. [3]

For the Latin liturgy was the vehicle of a culture, a foreign culture composed of Roman, Greek, and Jewish elements. And it was imposed by the new barbarian leaders, either for political reasons or from a sense of inferiority. In any case, it was no product of the people, of their native genius. They and their tribal inheritance had no voice, not a chance, in the high councils of an emergent 'Christendom.'

So the alien culture was imposed and adopted. If the assimilation betrayed some signs of wayward indigenous survivals or typical developments, these were arrested, banned from the liturgy, driven forth to fare for themselves. These expulsions occurred just as the people were about to add something of their own, were about to participate in the Latin culture and liturgy (so entwined.)

What might Western European music have become, minus centralizing movements like the Carolingian renaissance, which sacrificed Gallican chant and threatened the liturgies of Milan and Benevenuto for the sake of political unification? Or, without the papal efforts, through the monks of Cluny, which replaced the Mozarabic churchsong in Spain with Roman music? Or, without the exclusion of perhaps 12,000 original mass Sequences by the Council of Trent? Or, without the Counter Reformation, which put an early end to the movement (predating the Reformation) for a vernacular liturgy?

How might liturgical music itself have developed, without these and many other drastic interventions, all of them motivated by distinctly extra-musical purposes?

This much is clear:  as a phenomenon of musical creativity, the Latin liturgical music gradually declined from the moment when the Council of Trent opted for the past, tried to hold fast to the thought and sensibility of the Middle Ages, and to fend off the unmistakable development (remember that the Church never recognized non-Gregorian music as her own).  The development went on, naturally, outside the Church, which at most merely kept track of it.  In itself, this emancipation of the profane was not a bad thing; but the absence of musical creativity within the Church was a symptom of stagnation there.

But what did this profane music become?  Unfortunately, its makers continued the bent it had brought out of the Church with it:  no real participation by the people.  It was made for a silent audience, while others 'entertained' them by singing or playing, attending to what the performers and composers had put together.  It was but a short jump to 'art for art's sake,' to program music, even to so-called 'confession' music.

In the West, unlike elsewhere in the world, the cultural music is *not* the folk music.  No, Western folk music is the music of the *Grundschicht*, of the unlettered people.  But apace with democratic thought elsewhere in the world, there arose among the common people relatively new and independent forms of music:  jazz, for example, and the so-called popular music which followed it like wildfire, everywhere.  Popular music has become an enormously lucrative business simply because the demand of the people, especially the young, is insatiable.

What if, what if — if the Latin liturgy had not imposed itself?  if, as in Antioch, Greece, Alexandria, Ethiop-

ia, it had been handmaid to the languages and folk music
of the people? Why are such questions worth raising here?

Not to learn about the past, as such, but to learn
about the present, and to find perspective and inspiration
for the future, by focusing in upon our own potential and
that of our music. For, in fact, folk music is generally unknown territory for the Western professional musician. He
feels, furthermore, that he is at least a good whole rung
above it. He cannot imagine folk music which is 100 per-
cent music; in Western Europe, at least, he has probably
never encountered genuinely good folk music.

Thus, he would be surprised, in the Balkans today,
to hear a music so rhythmically complicated that he could
scarcely produce it, however professional he may be —
even though Balkan folk musicians turn it out spontaneously and the people dance to it with perfect ease. And
as for vocal embellishing techniques, how much our professional singers have yet to learn from Spanish and Arabian
folk music! We are just beginning to realize these enormous possibilities.

I am reminded, concretely, of the astounding improvi-
sations which I heard from the drummer accompanying
Sammy Davis, Jr. If I compare his feat with the famous
drum solo of Stockhausen, *Cycle for a Percussionist*, I must
honestly pronounce the latter mere child's play. And what
I heard could only have been improvisation. Scored, it would
have looked like the *Sacre du Printemps* for one player,
rather than for 135!

In a later context, I shall treat of vocality and vocal
ornamentation.[4] Here I would but note the following:
when one knows how to make the most of speech sounds
as a means of musical expression — which Western professional singers do not know — instead of using them merely
as an occasion for vocalization, then one gains control of

a variety of sounds compared to which serial instrumenta-
tion technique loses interest, and electronic music tastes
like synthetic food.  Some electro-musicians, like Herbert
Eimert, have made this discovery as they manipulated
fixed speech sounds on tape.

Practically every part of the world except Western
Europe testifies that folk music can, indeed, be music in
the fullest sense of that word.  And the professional musician will become increasingly receptive to the idea once
he realizes that Western Europe simply lacks anything like
a developed folk music, for quite non-musical reasons.  He
must learn to believe in the possibility of folk music of
the highest quality, despite its discouraging history in one
sector of the world.  Church music has, in fact, some discouraging pages which, nonetheless, are instructive for
grasping its present predicament — and ours.

## III. DISCOURAGING FACTS

In 578, the Council of Auxerre forbad women to sing
in church.  Granted, this was but a local Council, and Curt
Sachs is too sweeping when he states, flatly, that 'the Church'
issued such a prohibition (cf. *Our Musical Heritage*, Prentice-
Hall, New York, 1955).  Still, it did reflect the general thinking of the time.  For centuries, women were not admitted to
sing in the choirs, which can only be attributed to a marked
apprehension about sex, reflected in even the most recent
Church documents.[5]   They could sing as part of the general congregation, which meant rarely enough.  Perhaps their
talents went into the folk music, beyond the ecclesial walls.
For nearly 1500 years, then, half the population was excluded from even the minimal role of the elite choir, reserved
for boys and men.  As for composing, women have been a
rare phenomenon there, until this century.

During those same 1500 years, the Church strove to undermine every contribution of the Germanic peoples to Church music. Here I am indebted to the orthodox Catholic historian, Gustav Fellerer (cf. his *The History of Catholic Church Music*[6]), for the main points I shall make. [7]

Pope Gregory I (reigned 590-604) grasped the importance of a uniform liturgy for the position of Rome in the universal Church. Helped by the growth of the Merovingian dynasty, he set about producing a uniform Church music (*op. cit.*, p. 29) by founding the *Schola Cantorum* at Rome. This act prevented change in Church music by way of free improvisation (p. 30).

An important step was the official adoption of the Gregorian liturgical song, in use at Rome, [8] as an instrument for unifying and centralizing — a phenomenon of the general political scene in Europe at that time (p. 31).

Fellerer describes the opposition which was experienced in areas that had developed their own reading of the liturgical song. The Ambrosian liturgy had to give way here and there at the command of the Pope, but generally it managed to survive the pressure from Rome, although it became limited to an even smaller area (p. 31).

The Gallican liturgy felt this strong pressure from Rome, as also from Pepin and, later, Charlemagne. This liturgy, as used in southern France and in Spain, displayed, via Gothic influence, clear Greek-Byzantine traces. Later, Moorish elements enriched it, to produce the so-called Mozarabic liturgy.

Late in the 8th century, and despite strong popular resistance, the Church moved to 'coordinate' this liturgy with the Roman liturgy. Both Church and State saw this as a part of forming a strong, unified Europe and Rome. By the 11th century, Pope Gregory VII, supported by King Alphonsus of Castille, could celebrate the triumph of Roman liturgical song in Spain (p. 32).

In England, Rome faced a quite different situation. There, among a notably musical people, a pre-Gregorian liturgy flourished, introduced long since by Christian Roman legionnaires — and preserved still in the so-called *Sacramentarium Bonifacianum*. To strengthen Roman ties and influence, Pope Gregory I dispatched Abbot Augustine and companions in 596, several centuries of liturgical freedom later! And in 747, the Council of Glasgow decreed the formal adoption of the hymnal prescribed by Rome — and indeed, freshly delivered to the assembled Fathers by courier. Thus, it would be a thoroughly Romanized liturgy which English missionaries would carry to the Germanic lands (p. 32).

Among the Franks, there was an even stronger pre-Gregorian tradition of song. The preference for Gregorian exercised by Pepin and Charlemagne was politically motivated. In Metz, Bishop Chrodegang (held office 742-760) founded a school of music which became a center of Gregorian. The Emperor Charles set up a similar school, the *Schola Palatina*, at Aachen. But powerful popular opposition to the Roman imposition led Charlemagne to modify his plans for total Gregorianization, and he appointed the Deacon Paul, c. 790, and the Englishman Alcuin, c. 800, to effect some kind of musical compromise (p. 33).

In Germany, the introduction of the new liturgical melodies a century later led to countless local adaptations, especially in the northern cities of Trier, Cologne, Münster, and Mainz, where peculiar melodic forms lived on into the 19th century. In southern Germany, the 8th century missionaries came upon an old Christian liturgy, dating from the Roman colonists and incorporating Germanic tribal elements, which survived until the Council of Trent erased it in favor of the Gregorian liturgy (p. 33).

The Romanization process relied heavily on pivotal centers for its Gregorian campaign, notably the abbeys of Reichenau and, especially, St. Gallen. The latter, as we

now are aware, was not so much a center for new Gregorian
song as it was for handing on the Roman imports, and for
arbitrating conflicts with local recalcitrants whose adaptations can be traced down to the present (p. 34).

These adaptations reached between the indigenous
musical culture and the essentially alien importations produced, in the 9th century, several new forms. The first and
most important of these was the *trope*, in which a newly
written text (Latin and clerical) was distributed beneath
a melismatic tune in such wise that one syllable stood under each note of the melisma. Such a procedure has some
significant implications for our total context. First, it means
that the tonsured sons of the people did not know how to
sing the very melismas which had been imposed upon them.
Yet they could not free themselves from it interiorly. Then,
note, the trope form froze absolutely fast the reading, the
progression and number of notes, in the melisma — which
is, by its nature, meant for free, improvised ornamentation.
Bound to these untouchable melodies, the local churches
tried to render them more meaningful by writing new texts
for them, suited to the season or expressing local insights.
But try as they may, the melody took precedence over its
meaning, especially where no one knew what to do with
the melody itself (pp. 37-38).

Another new form was the *sequence*, originally a kind
of troping of the 'alleluia-jubilus.' But it did not remain such
very long, for the melody was soon expanded. And so the
sequences emerged as independent compositions, with forms
quite different from the rest of the Gregorian repertoire,
which constitutes them an important witness of autochtho-
nous music in the 10th to 13th centuries (pp. 39-40), as
were, also, the *cantiones* — invariably set to Latin texts,
but sung outside of liturgy (p. 40).

*A portion of the Kyrie-Trope Omnipotens, by Tutilo (Tenth Century, St. Gallen):*

1. Om - ni - po - tens   ge - ni - tor,   De - us   om -

ni - um   cre - a - tor:   e -

lei - son.

*A portion of the Sequence Christus hunc diem, by Nokter Balbulus (Tenth Century, St. Gallen):*

1. Chri - stus   hunc   di - em   jo - cun - dum   cun - ctis

con - ce - dat   es - se   Chri - sti - a - nis

a - ma - to - ri - bus   su - is.

The first traces of singing in the vernacular date back to the 8th century. Fellerer mentions German texts which were added after the *Kyrie* of the All Saints liturgy, for extra-liturgical use, of course. A *Kyrie* trope, in German, was used in Prague in the 10th century. The oldest example of a German church-song is the *Freisinger Petruslied*, 9th century. In 1148, Gerloh von Reichersberg alludes to vernacular songs in praise of the Savior which are sung in the whole world, especially in Germany. These included not only translations of tropes, sequences, and hymns, but completely new vernacular texts, due in part to the musical genius of the troubadours, the trouvères, and the Minnesänger. Strophe and rhyme now became the determinants of form, with colloquial style. From the 13th century onward, the melodies are more and more in the musical language of the people (pp. 41-43).

Liturgical drama, first in Latin, and then from the 12th century also in the vernacular, bears witness not only to verbal creativity, as the trope did, nor only to musical creativity as it appeared in the sequences and *cantiones*, but also to the power of ritual form, to the capacity for designing a completely new 'rite.' From the 11th century, these liturgical dramas were widely performed.

The oldest were the Easter plays, followed by the shepherd's play for Christmas, the Magi play, then a Rachel play, a *sponsus* play — about the wise and the foolish virgins, and a Daniel play. These mystery plays served to put the liturgy and the sermons in a form intelligible to the people, a form evoking and expressing their own faith. And so they were gradually pushed out the church door (pp. 43-44).

Western Europe went on trying to express itself in word and music at its liturgies, next by polyphonic music. We cannot here trace its whole development, but from its first appearance in the 9th century, it maintained for hundreds of years the original Gregorian melodies, thereby

proving again how untouchable these were. However, the
more these melodies failed to speak for themselves, the
less they satisfied.

Church authorities obstructed polyphony by the de-
cree *Docta SS. Patrum* of Pope John XXII, in 1324-25 (to
be reaffirmed by the Council of Trent) that the Latin texts
should be so sung as to be intelligible!  Such pleas really
meant that, outside of Rome, people paid little attention
to the texts, except to embellish them with the most beautiful  music they could devise.  Thus, polyphony became a
kind of *avant la date*; the only way to make the liturgy
say anything to the people was to give it a polyphonic setting.

The brief historical survey made here serves to indicate how persistently and sedulously Rome intervened and
blocked the people's attempts at religious musical expression
in Western Europe.  The liturgy was Latin, of, for, and almost entirely by clerics, composed by them until well into
the 16th century.  The vernacular was banned.  But when
it did gain official acceptance 'beyond the pale,' history
attests how richly it contributed to the development of
language, e.g., in Luther's translation of the Bible, the
Dutch *Statenbijbel*, and the Old Slavonic translations.  Until very recently, the vernacular never had a chance in the
Roman Church.

The meaning is clear, however painful:  from the beginning, the Western Church simply showed no respect for
the natural musical contribution of the peoples whom she
sought to Christianize.  Whenever folk musicality tried to
raise its head and voice in Church, it was neutralized and
eradicated by specialized musicians and clerics who went
on conducting their liturgy before a largely silenced people.

Western musicality made its way, nonetheless, under
other auspices, outside the Church, outside 'Christendom,'

and granted the enormous influence of Roman Catholicism
in that kingdom, we see here a proof of an enormous vitality in that music.


## IV. SOME ENCOURAGING FACTS


The professional musician and music historian may
be inclined to conclude that the West has not only never
possessed a highly developed folk music, but that it is now
too late for any such thing to appear.

But the vitality I allude to, demonstrated precisely by
Western folk musicality in its long struggle with Rome, has
convinced me that it is not too late. History attests to that
vitality. True, the musical phenomena I shall adduce do not
fall directly under the concept of folk music. But my con-
tention is this: the source of these phenomena, of these
professional cultural developments, is none other than folk
musicality itself. In other words, the professionals drew
from their own cultural environment, and in so doing, they
drew from the folk music inextricably lodged there.

I adduce, and shall briefly discuss, four phenomena:

A. Gregorian chant

B. polyphony

C. the fruitfulness of Protestant church music

D. the influence of folk music upon profane


### A. Gregorian Chant

In Gregorian chant, one can distinguish a Romance
from a Germanic dialect: in certain formulas, the (probable)
original Roman 'b' gradually changed, to 'b-flat' in the

Gallic lands or to 'c' in the Germanic lands. This indicates
not only a breakthrough by Western understanding, but
also a Western influence on the final form of the melodies.
And it shows a Western preference for major and minor,
much accentuated later on. The feeling for modality was
weak in the West, but so was its feeling for Gregorian
rhythm, which eventually was simply lost, to be replaced
by a feeling for tactus, meter, and, later, for measure.
A certain tactus was probably there and at work in the
Sequences, which, despite the Tridentine prohibition,
certainly made an important contribution to the development of the song, as did the liturgical drama to the
theatre and opera.

### B. Polyphony

Polyphony, as the term is used in the West, is found
nowhere else in the world, nor in the entire history of music. Pioneered in liturgical music, meeting many difficulties
there, as noted, it has nonetheless continued to develop
right up to the present.

Can polyphony tell us anything about folk music?
Off hand, one is inclined to say no, since by and large it
is not 'folk.' It found a place in the liturgy, in the gap
created by the absence of the monks and the silence of
the people (the choir would fill it later). Far from being
'folk,' it actually worked against the people's participation.[9]

But did the people experience it this way? They
only knew how to look and listen: the liturgy spoke of
a world different from their own; the choir represented
the heavenly voices of the hereafter. The people were
perhaps quite content with that dream.[10]

Polyphony definitely did not depend for its unique-
ness on Rome, on Gregorian chant or the Latin in the

liturgy. It came, rather, from the grass-roots and answered the needs of the silent people.

A few phases in the development of this polyphony: the use of thirds, most likely taken over from the Norsemen; the use of fourths and fifths; the motet, which developed in the direction of the madrigal and the polyphonic chanson; the development of the major and minor tonal system; the development of rhythm via modal rhythm toward meter and measure; the discovery of the bass function in the *basso seguente*, later the *basso continuo* which opened out into the concept of the functional bass. Note, too, how much the composition of polyphonic Masses owes to chansons borrowed from folk music in so-called chanson-Masses, at least from Dufay up to and including Palestrina.

## C. The Fruitfulness of Protestant Church Music

With the advent of the Reformation, Protestant Church music made a fresh start with folk music. It also availed itself of the first vernacular psalms, produced in fact just before the break. Both Luther and Calvin took a stand for the people's right to sing in the liturgy, the latter making simply no place for a professional choir. Schuetz, Buxtehude, J. S. Bach, and other composers developed this folk musicality, but — once more — gave it a professional, non-popular direction, conditioned as they were by their own musical history. But the product was powerful, distinctly superior to the development taking place in France, Spain, and Italy, whose Latin liturgy was deprived of this healthy injection. The English people were learning to sing together with a polyphonic choir, notably their much loved Christmas carols. To this practice one can directly trace a work like Elgar's *Land of Hope and Glory*.

## D. The Influence of Folk Music upon Profane

From the time that one can distinguish a profane or
secular culture, about the time of the Council of Trent,
folk music has exercised a continuous influence. From
the time of the oldest chanson-Masses to the present, we
find variations composed upon folk songs. The return to
simplicity by Bach's progeny and by the composers of the
Mannheim school is marked by a clear folk tendency.
Haydn stands, in many ways, close to folk music. Folk
songs influenced the development of *Singspiel* in opera.

The rise of the important 'national' schools of the
19th century should remind us, in our context, that they
took their nationality precisely from the special character
of their folk music. These nations lay like a circle around
the heart of Europe,[11] and were less urbanized and less
Latinized than the countries they surrounded. In some
of these areas on the periphery of Europe a vernacular
liturgy had even been used.

In the late Romantic period composers like Mahler
sought inspiration in folk songs. Debussy's encounter with
Javan folk music was a decisive influence in his development.
Bartók made himself a disciple of folk music. The basic
motif of Stravinsky's *Sacre du Printemps* (D flat - B flat -
E flat - B flat) sounds exactly like the opening of a famous
Russian folk song.[12]

**Notes — Chapter Three**

1. Compare, for example, the importance of a single official translation of the Bible, for a variety of national dialects. See p. 60.

2. Compare p. 64.

3. i.e., had it even been possible to think in such terms.

4. See pp. 95-97.

5. See the Instruction *Musicam Sacram*, no. 23; the encyclical *Musicae Sacrae*, no. 36; the Instruction *De Musica Sacra et de Liturgia*, no. 100.

6. Karl Gustav Fellerer, *The History of Catholic Church Music* (Helicon Press, Baltimore, 1961).

7. For corrections and refinements, see the article by Joseph Smits van Waesberghe, "Einleitung zu einer Kausalitätserklärung der Evolution der Kirchenmusik im Mittelalter (von etwa 800 bis 1400)," in *Archiv für Musik-Wissenschaft*, 1969, pp. 249-275. He discusses questions very like my own, though there is no mutual dependence.

8. Here I prefer to omit discussion of the 'old Roman' Gregorian.

9. See p. 109, f.

10. See pp. 111-113.

11. Compare pp. 48-49.

12. See p. 89, f.

# Chapter Four

## Artistic Integrity in Composing Liturgical Music in the Vernacular

### I. LOSS

Must part of the cost of introducing the vernacular into our liturgy be music of a lower standard? One is justified in being uneasy on this score, at the very least. The new liturgy would seem to involve a series of losses, namely:

A. loss of function

B. loss of repertoire

C. loss of quality

D. loss of contact with contemporary secular music.

### A. Loss of Function

Before the Second Vatican Council, the Latin rite was quite unalterably fixed. The sung Mass was conducted according to rubrics which had been established for centuries. It precisely prescribed a series of liturgical actions and texts

which could be accompanied by instrumental music or which
had to be sung. Organ literature abounds with titles like
'Offertory,' 'Elevation,' 'Communion,' 'Benediction.' And
the rite guaranteed that these pieces could be performed.
Some texts belonged to the 'ordinary' of the Mass, others
to the 'proper' — and the setting of the latter was generally
from the Gregorian repertoire. Many choirs found this
difficult music. But even though complete success might
elude them, they were in constant contact with a repertoire
of the highest order.

In the performance of the 'ordinary,' one could draw
upon the musical literature of many centuries. The selections might vary in quality, and the performance; but the
obligation to sing certain sections assured an important
place to music, and it could, of course, be done with great
distinction.

But this inevitably fixed the function of the music,
too. In such a list of prescribed times, pieces, etc., composers forgot to ask themselves what should be the particular function of a piece of music at a particular point in the
entire liturgy. Like picnickers along a roadside, they were
grateful for the spots afforded them, and settled down
there. In our time, the importance of specific function
has been fruitfully explored by Joseph Gelineau, among
others. [1]

Fortunately, the Second Vatican Council has opened
up possibilities for adapting the liturgical rite to the requirements of a genuinely renewed liturgy, thus ending the long
immutability of that rite. For, in making a set of changes,
the Council has, as I judge, opened the way to others. Who
can really believe, by the whole tenor of that Council, that
all has been fixed now for the next many centuries?

On the contrary, liturgy has now entered upon a continuing process of self-renewal quite incompatible with fixed
prescriptions like "at this point, this person or group will

sing exactly this selection." No, neither the composer nor the choir nor the people will hereafter find a rite to which the music must relate just so, in which its function is, once for all, defined, established, fixed.

And so, the question of the function of the music at every point in the liturgy is now a prime one, and the criterion for the making of that music is now changed. It is no longer to accompany prescribed actions and to interpret prescribed texts. The new criterion, I believe, is this: will this music, used here in the service, invite, promote, and (musically) compel the active participation of the people? That is now the prime consideration.

### B. Loss of Repertoire

An obvious but important fact: when the vernacular replaces Latin in the liturgy, the entire Latin repertoire disappears. This means, in the first place, the end of Gregorian, despite more or less defensible efforts to salvage bits of it by reworking them into new vernacular songs. The repertoire as a whole, as it has grown and functioned, will be lost.

This applies, also, to all those other compositions, to Guillaume de Machaut, the Notre Dame school, to all the polyphony from Dufay through Palestrina, to Monteverdi, the 17th century French composers. Allow me to continue the list, to indicate the full measure of this loss: Haydn, Mozart, Beethoven, Schubert, Liszt, Bruckner, Caplet, Andriessen, Badings, Poulenc, Litaize, Jenny, Heiller, Schroeder, van Nuffel, de Vocht, Kodály, and Stravinsky. And others!

In the face of such a loss, due not to the renewers but to the ecclesiastical conservatism of centuries, a great deal must transpire, obviously, to render the change from Latin to the vernacular acceptable to the musician.

### C. Loss of Quality

If one agrees in principle that the people should take part in the singing, and even accepts their performance as a criterion (which, in a vernacular liturgy, it is), then one can no longer demand concert-level musical quality, obviously. Indeed, discounting the few minutes often allowed for it, which is simply not serious work, we must say that the people do not rehearse in the new situation.[2] Were the people truly to rehearse, they would become 'a choir.' The people are going to have to find their participation (and pleasure, it is hoped) in their own unprofessional performance! Which raises, no doubt, serious questions about the quality of that performance.

But here I would have you recall what I have said earlier about the composer's need for a 'conversion' and about the need for an elementary music. And I would raise this prior question: what should be the kind and quality of the new compositions, designed, I would hope, not for concert halls, not for 'professionals,' but for the sung participation of 'the people.'

A congregation which does not really rehearse, is musically unskilled — is it possible that a modern composer would be prepared to compose for them, with all their limitations taken fully into account? Or does such a task exceed, in fact, the limits of his very professionalism? Is the writing of songs 'simple enough' for them such a simple task, after all?

Recall what has happened. During the last century a virtuosity developed that permitted the composer to make the highest technical demands, and freed him to write whatever he felt he must write. In our century, this freedom expanded with the discarding of all fixed rules of harmony and counterpoint, the new system of notation, the advent of electronic music — with its whole new range of sounds.

The limitations imposed on the composition of the required liturgical song seem diametrically opposed to that great degree of freedom. They seem to condemn the composer to *Gebrauchsmusik* [3] in the worst sense. Or to 'entertainment' music, completely focused on the people. Such concerns have been so widespread that I would like to speak to them, once again. [4]

Briefly, entertainment music is composed for ease of *listening*, elementary music for ease of *performing*. The people find it much more difficult to perform the songs they listen to for their entertainment. They can manage only much simpler songs, and this is why the composer is compelled toward elementary music — the last thing one would find in entertainment music. The latter is hardly ever folk music, as defined in Chapter One. If one doubts the great challenge to the composer in the composition of 'simple,' elementary music, he need only try it! My own efforts refute the fear that the liturgical music thereby produced must suffer in quality. The achievement of this kind of genuine simplicity (far removed from anything jejune) is, I can attest, an enormously difficult enterprise.

### D. Loss of Contact with Contemporary Secular Music

Since the time of the Council of Trent, and notably since the Cecilianism of the last century, the development of church music has lagged behind that of secular music. The 19th century was characterized by the neo-styles. To that extent, the ideal of a Palestrina renaissance had not yet become so unacceptable. Indeed, composers and directors took delight in a derivative of his style to assure easy execution by amateur choirs. Composers like Alphons Diepenbrock were understandably exasperated by those who seemed to think the clock could stand still for church music, that a church musician could afford to remain aloof from the development of style in his own times —

a stance even less palatable today. What an ordeal for
a contemporary composer to write music not intended
to be 'contemporary'!

Nonetheless, if one would compose music for the
liturgical participation and singing of people today, it is
evident that he cannot compose today's contemporary
music. For one thing, as said before, the people at large
cannot sing it. Does this mean such a composer cannot,
in principle, be contemporary? Logically, it would seem
so. Unless, beyond all the losses, there is something he
may gain, some contribution he may make to the contemporary, the secular.

## II. A NEW MUSICAL SITUATION

The practice of church music is in no danger of dis-
appearing from the musical scene. On the contrary, it
has great and unsuspected possibilities for development
in the quite new situation, I believe. It has lost something,
undoubtedly, in repertoire especially. But what can re-
place it is so important and offers such opportunity that,
on balance, I would speak of profit rather than loss, even
for secular music (cf. *infra*, III, Progress).

Before demonstrating this bold assertion, I wish to
compare the new musical situation with the old, to provide
a better understanding of the change we are dealing with.

Common to both situations is a triangular arrangement:
Composer − Choir (& instrumentalists) − People (& priest).
Each of these influences and helps to define the others, of
course; each is, in measure, both independent and dependent.
But the older situation was, in fact, like this: the Composer
functioned as Source, the Choir as Middle-Man, the People

as Consumer. In these terms, the new situation has drastically altered the People's role and function, and this fact has profound effect upon all of them.


### A. The Composer

In the older situation, the composer found his basic goal and motive in self-expression. His effort aimed to express, in musical terms, what he felt about the religious event in general (e.g., awe for the holy) and about a given text or action to be accompanied, in particular. He expressed his reaction, and his musical expression was to be performed. If he observed a few limits − not too long, avoid dance rhythms, respect the text − he was free to write the music he considered beautiful. Could it be performed? That was not really his concern; that was the choir's concern.

He was occupied principally with this task: to translate into music whatever appeared in the Latin text. The earlier Gregorian composer had, at least, the challenge to create the musical possibility for *singing the text in an expressive manner.* But this was not, in general, a norm for subsequent composers. [5]

The reason should be quite obvious: his intended audience could not have understood the Latin texts, no matter how expressively he composed their music. Until this century, there were not even Latin/vernacular translations. The choir was in the same boat, and one may wonder whether many composers were not half-way in it, too. The choir may have taken great pains with proper pronunciation and enunciation − that was still a far cry from understanding what they were singing. In such a situation, the people were content with very sketchy comprehension, and the musical settings posed no higher demands.

The new situation, entailing vernacular texts, is clearly very different for all concerned. The composer has a task at once easier and harder — he can more easily express his own language, but now for a much more demanding choir and people, especially since the latter are now to sing it, in much larger measure, at least.

Specifically, he must meet these demands:

1. He must attune his ear with extraordinary care to the exact *sound* of the people's singing, and to the relation between this sound and that of the choir. As we say, he must learn to 'write for the instrument,' the sound of the people.

2. He must adapt his composing to their technical possibilities. This requires, as described earlier, a clear idea of elementary musicality.

3. He must accomodate his composition, as far as he is able, to the tastes of the people, with musical settings so suited to the 'folk' that they are inspired to participate. This means music and texts they find it psychologically possible to make their own because they enable their own self-expression (no longer just his), or at least the expression of the communal self we call the 'congregation.' Formerly, he gave them his interpretation of the text; now he must so compose that they can give their interpretation, expressing it with the help of his music.

### B. The Choir

In the older situation, the task of the classical church choir was interpretation of what the composer had dreamt and captured in notes. The choir (or director) might choose its repertoire according to its own tastes and skill, but their

job was to convey to the listeners their own experience of
the composer's creation. Their role was that of the middle-
man, the mid-wife, in service to text, music, composer, and
audience. Their art was for listening to, for being heard.
Their criteria: a good selection, well interpreted, and well
performed.

The choir's task today does not exclude these elements,
but the new situation may be said to transform them by
transforming the basic function of the choir itself. For now
the liturgical celebration must be, in the first place, an act
of the whole community, priest and choir and people all
actively participating, and in this context, the task of the
choir is *to set in motion, promote, and support the liturgical act of the whole assembled community.*

"Active participation" does not do real justice to the
people's role (neither does 'role' – the whole matter is hob-
bled by a terminology itself waiting transformation). It
is not as though, having settled the role of the celebrant
and the role of the choir, one must say, O yes, what can
be found for the people to do, since they are to 'actively
participate'? Given texts and music which embody the
indivisible character of the liturgical act itself, the choir's
task will be to inspire the people to sing, to want to sing,
in their turn, even to be impatient for their turn! (with
many consequences for the execution, e.g., crescendos and
decrescendos subordinated to a dynamic articulation.)

The classical choir had no such task. It could possibly
move the listeners interiorly (if it did not confine itself to
moving and praising the Lord), it perhaps teased them by
provoking the desire to do, to be actively engaged in what
was going on, but none of this matches what is now asked
of the people. Heretofore, if they cooperated, it was in
listening, in attending, and their main advance had been
to get out from behind the choir screen. The attention
fell upon the altar, and upon the religious event before
(and somehow above) their eyes. But today, what takes

place within the community at liturgy, among people, has
assumed equal, even primary importance.

Thus, today's choir is less a center of rapt listening,
more a group who announce the cheers so compellingly
that the whole stadium follows their lead, resoundingly,
and they all join in, even those up around the table.

### C. The People

As we have seen, in church music old style, the people
were listeners.  They could not translate into their own sound
or movement what they were undergoing, what they experienced (in or out of the church precincts).  They had been
schooled to silence by the Latin rite (if you want to know
what that is like, just sit in on a 'music appreciation' class
at a typical high school).  This defined the roles of composer and choir, of course; the attitude of the people con-
ferred clear priority and attention upon them.  Those who
were trained to listen went to church to hear a mass by
Mozart or Palestrina; they could not have thought of going
there for each other, to become a people, to make and
celebrate their community by sharing in and through Jesus,
and thus to begin, at least, to experience themselves as,
in fact, the people of God.

Their plight was not really relieved by a theory of the
Eucharistic Sacrifice (much less by one of table-fellowship!).
They knew as little theology as Latin, and would have been
quite astounded to learn what, by some theologies, was supposed to be transpiring in the church.  Yes, they did hear
beautiful music, at times, with the sense of awe for the holy
which it can produce, even in so-called pagan rites.

Today, as has been said above, the people themselves
are at the center of the liturgy.  Composer and choir are
still important, but secondary.  The people no longer sit
back and evaluate what these have produced.  The produc-

tion belongs to the whole assembly. It is their experience.
That is the event.

They used to demand 'originality' of the composer.
Now they want him to write music they can perform and
find appealing, suited to their technical and psychological
capabilities. If he is inventive, they pay him with admiration. But they ask, above all, that he not exclude them,
not add to their already considerable sense of powerless-
ness, a feeling which numbs and deadens interest and
participation.

## III. PROGRESS

Here I propose to briefly survey and assess the profit
and loss entailed in the transition from the old to the new
situation of church music, a matter touched upon before.

### A. The People

As detailed above, they can no longer listen in church
to the masterpieces of the classical repertoire. Possibly the
vernacular liturgy will yield its own masterpieces, in time.
But they will not come readily, within the limits set by
the need to integrate the singing of the general community.
And the elementary character of their part, while not excluding a degree of greater technical complexity in parts
assigned to the choir, will still exercise some measure of
restraint throughout the composition. People long used
to passive listening to what moves the composer and the
choir will certainly experience this loss all the more.

But their big gain is evident: they become co-performers, music-makers. However elementary, their active participation seems to me clear progress, and clearly preferable to

mere listening. At times, moreover, they can still listen to
the choir 'stealing the show,' because they know it will be
returned to them, that their own participation in the liturgy
is almost always experienced as the high point. And, to
anticipate a bit, the choir itself gains by the new outward
embodiment of the people's response to them.

Concert hall music and singing might well ponder this
point. For example (if one may add a gloss to sacred pages),
who should really sing the simple melody, *Alle Menschen
werden Bruder*, in the finale to Beethoven's Ninth Symphony?
Choir and orchestra intertwine to express what the listeners
feel. Why do the listeners, the people in the hall, not express
and sing their own feelings? What could be more natural,
in place of their listening to the 'development.'[6]  Would
not both choir and orchestra gain much from this response
and embodiment?

Indeed, the avant-garde today is pursuing such possibilities of 'audience participation' — certainly in theatre. In
how many ways might a renewed people's liturgy once more
inspire and enrich the secular, profane arts, even music?

## B. The Choir

In the new church music, the choir — professionals,
semi-professionals, skilled amateurs — still functions to elicit
the full interior, spiritual participation of the people, but
now pointed toward its actual and quite audible expression.
To make this further goal truly the climax, embodiment,
and expression of their own musical intention and activity
requires a significant degree of self-effacement on their
part. They share the billing now, to say the least. Every-
body is not always listening to them. Will the choir experience this as gain or loss? That depends upon their actual
priorities.

The choir sings in church, true. But quite often, especially if they are not professionals, they have a strong
need to reproduce the aura of the concert hall. Amateurs
may well feel unequal to the new musical situation, and
harbor a sense that their new role betokens the small esteem
in which their performance is held.

These problems, in somewhat different ways, confront
others involved, also, the composer, the celebrants, the instrumentalists. The transition to a people's liturgy involves,
as said earlier, a genuine conversion, of values, attitudes,
priorities — and this can be painful. The entire community,
and especially its leadership (here, the director) must work
through the fears, sensitivities, and human growth problems
involved in all communal life. The decisive help, for all,
will be the experience of the new liturgy itself, as it creates
the sense of mutual need and support which breaks old
molds, makes new people.

### C. The Composer

The old-style composer may feel quite at a loss in the
new situation, for he is really being asked to become a new
kind of musician. Often, he may be unwilling or unable.
But we cannot blink the fact: the new music needed requires
a new musician. Can he summon up the courage, the flexi-
bility such a situation demands? Or will he just fade away,
in favor of newer, younger composers?

The problem of the old-style composer, as I see it,
lies in his image of himself. Primarily, as composer, he
wants to be listened to, and he cannot or will not put
himself at the service of the elementary music of the people
because doing so would not agree with the image of musical functioning he has projected for himself. He is now
offered the chance to move away from that role, from

being listened to, and so to lift from himself the twin burden
the role has laid on him: the demand to be *original* and the
compulsion to be *contemporary*.

### Originality

The general musical climate, especially the avant-garde,
so opposed to, yet so influenced in that very opposition by,
Romanticism, exercises powerful pressure for originality. Only the very greatest composers, I fear, have resisted it. Sig-
nificantly, it enjoins him to *strive for originality*. But this,
I submit, is an injunction one would do well to ignore, as
it contains a self-contradiction, hence is self-defeating. I
can best show this by examples.

Along with fingerprints and photographs, handwriting
is one of the clearest proofs of identity. But the expert
looks precisely to the unstudied, unintentional, 'unstriven-for'
details, revealed in a sample not composed for his scrutiny.
Yet this highly personal and original thing we call our handwriting was, as we know, acquired precisely through the
laborious effort to imitate the writing of others, their hand
guiding our own.

Again, the practicing psychologist learns what is truly
original and significant about his client, not so much from
his studied responses as from the spontaneous, the involun-
tary and unconscious words, gestures, expressions. Here he
can get behind the impression the person strives to make,
the projected personality, to the fundamental, original one.

A last example: what is more original about a person
than his voice? his exact way of speaking? But here, again,
the process of learning was profoundly one of imitation;
remember those tiresome, endless corrections, "repeat after
me"! Striving to do exactly what another did, each person
came to a unique expression of himself. After that, all
striving for a particular effect sounds false, 'striven-for.'

Similarly, I believe, the composer will achieve original-ity only on condition of not consciously striving for it. If he rejects every likeness to others, his work will merit the Dutch saying that something or another "looks like nothing," meaning it is worth nothing. Because such an attempt is ultimately moved by a negation—a desire not to resemble.

Music critics have fed this desire to some extent, with their heavy emphasis upon tracing 'influences' in every work, often finding here a lack of musical personality, hence, of musical value. Thus the Western rationalism. But how should this norm apply to folk music, which loves to play with such ancient and universal formulas as sol—la—sol—mi?[7]

This wrongheaded pressure for a false originality de-rives, too from the traditional view of the composer as competitor. He must excel the others—all the performers, listeners, and everyone else. Notice that they are all thought of as his listeners—another effect of the long reign of the Latin liturgy.

Well, he is called today to freedom, really: to compose music the people can perform, so that remote, demanding listeners no longer hover always on his horizon, but are re-placed by active, joyous co-performers, nudging his pen.

### Contemporaneity

The other half of the burden borne by the old-style composer is the need to be 'contemporary.' What is 'con-temporary' has been dictated by a number of important musical compositions and a host of publications about them. One must meet their requirements of contemporaneity to be accepted as a composer, and if one does not speak their caste language, he is rejected as a pariah. But the composer who works at speaking that way will be just as cramped as he who strives to make himself original.

What, in fact, does 'contemporary' mean? It evades
easy definition because it has always to do with the present —
which is continually evolving.

I believe that man evolves, presses on, despite his
failures, and that it is good, and typically human, to be
aware of one's own development or evolution. With such
consciousness, man tries to take his existence into his own
hands, and part (at least) of that existence *is* evolution.
Thus, man strives to make the future and, *a fortiori*, the
present. Only in this sense, that he can 'make' his own
time, can he be called 'contemporary.'

But in the arts, I believe, one finds much more than
he makes. Within oneself, one happens upon things which
he does not control, cannot summon up on order. In some
sense, he is their guest, invited to partake of them. They
exceed him, and they trail inward further than he can reach.
How, for example, would parents set about making a pair
of eyes for their evolving child?

When I have composed with any success, I have always
had this distinct feeling that everything was already awaiting
me, and now I had chanced upon it, found it. Until then,
it lay there, no doubt, but I had always overlooked it.

And so I am thankful when I succeed. I have not so
much made something as found something. It was there,
but I was not. Perhaps my fellow-professionals and fellow-
seekers have helped me to look in the right place (in general,
they have not). I am contemporary, I believe, when I find
something now.

Or must I measure my contemporaneity by the quantity
of dissonances, flutter-tongues, tone-clusters? I have plenty
of those added in by the late arrivals at church, sitting down
with a clatter, coughing, proceeding boldly out of key! And
it is music to my ears, because it is unsanitized human sound

and human presence. They are all on our live tapes and recordings. At least, that much is allowed in church, if not
in the sacred concert hall, which is not designed for it, where
it is simply intolerable.

Maybe some contemporary composers are supplying
those sounds themselves, or letting the orchestra or soloist
do it. Maybe they need to break the intolerable tension,
the idolatrous and magical silence of the listening audience.
Far better, curses, cat-calls, and walk-outs. In a really thriv-
ing liturgy, in a true church community, those things take
care of themselves, quite unplanned, the sounds of life!

To be contemporary, to take one's existence into one's
own hands, even in this sense it entails a danger, i.e., to
stand on the tip of your toes to appear a little taller than
you are. Pushed a step higher, it becomes the effort to
compose works of 'timeless' value. But value is inseparable
from here and now, from these people who are to perform
or hear this work.

And the composer of the new liturgical music will
come to realize, as by a revelation, that it is better to for-
get the judgment of history and making the books, in favor
of serving the people all around him, helping them to the
happiness of participation. In time, this brings about a
gain in function, and a new repertoire; a gain in the quality
of both composition and performance — and, not least, a
life-giving contact with, a membership in, the contemporary
community. That, I submit, is contemporaneity *par excellence.*

**Notes – Chapter Four**

1. Joseph Gelineau, *Voices and Instruments in Christian Worship* (Liturgical Press, Collegeville, Minn., 1964).

2. See p. 22, f.

3. *Gebrauchsmusik*, literally, 'music for use'; functional music.

4. Compare p. 22, f.

5. See pp. 95-97.

6. See p. 6, f.

7. See p. 93, f. and p. 64.

*(Right) Bernard Huijbers directs the choir at the Dominicus-kerk, Amsterdam.*

# *Intermezzo*

In his book *Leven in Meervoud* ("Living in Plural")
J. H. van den Berg meditates upon the phenomenon of
photography (Callenbach, Nijkerk, 1963 – Eng. trans. in
preparation). His free-flowing selection has moved me
to offer the following reflections, transposed to the phenomenon of musical recordings – and vernacular liturgy.

*When one is being recorded*
*one plays or sings*
*just what the player or singer himself would like to hear.*
*He puts himself in place of the listener*
*and imagines how he*
*as listener*
*would like to hear it*
*and how as player he must play*
*to produce that effect in the listener.*

*This seems quite natural*
*but it makes for a complication.*
*The playing loses in artlessness and directness,*
*as though a woman*

*who knows that men gaze at her admiringly*
*were very artfully to make sure*
*she is seen as she wants to be seen,*
*even though they want to see her*
*not as she wants to be seen*
*but as she is.*

*People want to hear the player*
*not as he wants to be heard*
*but as he is.*
*That striving for effect*
*is not what they want to hear,*
*that trying to make a particular impression*
*intervenes between music and hearing.*
*One sees, one hears*
*the mirror-image, the double, the projection*
*muting the voice of the music*
*as affectation mutes a woman's beauty,*
*for beauty is artless.*

*Beauty looks out at us,*
*is gift, is grace,*
*is unearned experience,*
*whereas insight seizes things*
*and business instinct uses them*
*with power and cunning*
*for something beyond themselves.*
*Beauty does not impose or force itself*
*but is found,*
*happens to you,*
*is free gift.*

*No recording of the vernacular liturgy*
*sounds like being there.*
*One hears a record from outside,*
*a silent listener.*
*The people gathered in the church*
*listen but not silently;*

*their seeming silence is prelude*
*rich with expectation of their singing,*
*and they hear there in church*
*differently than someone hears a record,*
*and they go on to sing*
*as part of the entire community*
*which one who hears a record cannot do.*

*In true vernacular liturgy*
*all those music-makers*
*relate to each other differently*
*than concertizing musicians,*
*relate as before*
*the phonograph and tape recorder intervened.*

*Van den Berg asks*
*whether man relates differently*
*because photography has been invented,*
*and answers No,*
*the man who could relate by posing*
*for his picture*
*had changed before he could pose,*
*before photography,*
*had lost the gift of artlessness,*
*the courage to be artless, to be himself,*
*had learned to fear the impression he might make,*
*and so devised the photograph*
*for control.*

*And that was just the time*
*he began his controlling*
*and fixing of sound,*
*the time the musician became*
*over-sensitive to the impression*
*he was making on others,*
*unsure of himself*
*and afraid of them.*
*He lost artlessness*
*not because the phonograph was invented,*

*but the phonograph was invented
because he lost artlessness,
became arty,
which means afraid
of himself and the others,
began to control, censor, and edit
his image and sound.*

*A question to ponder:
does the new situation of church music
produce the new church musician,
or is that situation the product
of the new church musician,
changed by making music differently,
making music differently
because he has found a different way
to live and feel and be?*

*Is the man who makes music today
perhaps a new kind of man making a new kind of music,
unafraid to be artless and merely himself,
trusting and feeling safer with the other,
more at one with the other?*

*Does he announce
a new democracy,
freedom, equality,
a leap both fraternal and human?*

# Chapter Five

## Formula Technique and Vocality in the New Liturgical Folk Music (Half an Essay)

Michelangelo did not hesitate to deliver some of his sculptures half finished. And, according to one account, those were exactly the works he held dearest.

Though I imply no further comparison, this Chapter, too, is but half finished. The subject ought to have two whole chapters. I do not feel ready to write them, nor do I think they could be completed in our day, in any case. For the characteristics of the new liturgical music (and, I would hope, of all music) must emerge from praxis, not theorizing, and very much more praxis is needed. But I trust this half-essay will still have a certain value, as a sketch of two characteristics of the new liturgical folk music. I judge them very important, and they are often confused and misunderstood by musicians: *formula-technique* and *vocality*.

## I. FORMULA-TECHNIQUE

Folk music means variation on previously given formulas.  Let me cite again our Dutch cheering-song, sung
with such gusto in Amsterdam by the ardent fans of our
soccer team (Ajax): *Hij heeft gewonnen de zilvervloot.*[1]
This Dutch folk song is almost the identical melody found
in Tschaikovsky's Fourth Symphony, the latter being: *do–
la–re–do–(si)–do*.  The rest of the song is forgotten, but
this formula has endured like steel.  As is well known, it
may be found as a primal musical element in every time
and place in the world.[2]  When it sweeps through the
stadium, so strong is this collective call that accompaniment from a band or organ would be totally superfluous,
in fact a downright oddity!

In Western music, there are, of course, a variety of
techniques of variation (permit the redundancy!).  But most
of them vary the exact thing which remains constant in
folk music – the melos.  And formula-technique, a technique
of variation, leaves the melos unchanged.  In part, it is a
varying of rhythm, caused by the accents of the different
underlying texts; but mainly it consists in the endless timbre variation of ever changing vowels and consonants –
something instrument-oriented Western music scarcely even
notices.

For every vowel is, as it were, a different instrument;
and each consonant is something of a percussion instrument.
To the Western composer, steeped in the tradition we have
seen, it may well be shocking to suggest that his art develop
and be so determined by para-musical factors, i.e., by the
acoustical qualities of the language.  But are they really para-
musical?  Serial orchestration technique and electronic music
have taught us, I hope, that these sound-changes can very
well pertain to the domain of music proper.  They even
partly determine the character of the instruments.  But we
have not developed any new instruments for so long, and
have simply taken for granted the sound of those we have,

that we have, I believe, lost something of the feel for timbre variation.

## II. VOCALITY

I have become convinced that a fine sensitivity to the acoustical qualities of language is the basic element of genuine vocality. When we Western musicians speak of the 'typically vocal,' we think more in terms of melody forming than of timbre variation, more of larynx and cranial cavity than of articulation. But listening to Gregorian chant, especially as sung by the monks of Solesmes, has convinced me that vocality based on *pronunciation*, and hence on timbre variation, admits of untold possibilities of expression, beside which instruments simply pale. Is such a statement an exaggeration? For the listener, perhaps; but certainly, in my opinion, not for the performer, even allowing the factor of each one's subjective experience.

Thus understood, vocal expression will include an optimum degree of awareness and bodiliness. It contains and is motivated by a meaning, and this content is an inseparable part of the expression, not — as with an instrument — blind and a-conceptual. And yet, the conceptual content is exceeded by the intuitive bodiliness of breath, sung *speech*, lips, tongue. These are, in unison, something far beyond the mere 'voice' of a great singer.

The West, I believe, has largely forgotten this understanding of vocality. Is this part of the legacy of singing incomprehensible Latin for centuries? And is this not just the surprise of Solesmes, that we hear a choir of monks who have embodied the meaning in their Gregorian chant? And finally, is not this embodiment of meaning precisely what we miss in the rendition of so many well-meaning choirs who bend their voices fanatically to this unrivaled repertoire?

Not long ago, a Dutch radio network sponsored its own Gregorian schola. Even though they were professional singers, their performance simply lacked the vocality I am urging. Perhaps they had all specialized in vocal music of the period after classical polyphony, written more for the voice than for the word. One might say that it used the voice as just another instrument, with no regard to the acoustical qualities of the language itself.[3] That was the Italian opera, with its ideal of the *bel canto*. The recitative is incidental. The main thing is the aria, with its highly colored emotional effect. And the text of the aria, short and much repeated, can be rendered in other languages (as Handel did). Melody and voice – these were central.

Melody and voice: like instruments, so imitable upon instruments, e.g., *Blute nur*, from Bach's *Passion of Matthew*, played first on the flute. Recall (Chapter Two) my remarking the autonomy of the song – it, too, can be played.

Gregorian, in contrast, is a genuinely vocal conception, based on the timbre variations of language, on the quality of the words.[4] It cannot be performed instrumentally, any more than the music of Palestrina. Any ancient Gregorian melody loses its effectiveness if played, e.g., on the flute. Because such melodies were written not merely for the human voice (as, indeed, was *Blute nur*), but for the human *word*. But very little of the word element survives if one begins to treat the voice instrumentally, and if instrument oriented musicians are performing this music.

And so it has largely been, with Western European music. Our notation betrays it: developed for instrumental music, it has no notations for typically vocal effects. The instruments had few possibilities for timbre variation, if we except the flageolet tones, or playing *con sordino*, or on the G-string of the violin – and these could be indicated verbally or by less familiar signs only. The variations instruments dispose of, normally, are: *short-long, high-low, loud-soft, fast-slow*. But how, for example, is one to notate a

vocal accent which is not to be sung louder, but by shorten-
ing the vowel of the preparatory syllable? How does one
indicate a light accent?[5] No wonder our instrument oriented
composers are fond of placing the word accent on a relatively
heavy count or a longer note: on an instrument, there are
almost no other possibilities for normal accentuation. They
are constructed and used for tone-color stability, whereas
vocality, correctly understood, is based on tone-color variation.

That Western music has thought strongly in instrumental terms appears, also, in the terminology of form analysis.
Specifically, there is no term for the form of an ordinary
folk song; *song form* does not suit, as it means a piece of
instrumental music most easily compared to a song.

For vocal ornamentation, there are practically no notations. In any case, most Western vocalists are not in possess-
ion of its techniques, anyhow. Instrumental ornamentation
bears a slight resemblance to it, perhaps, or is derived from
it, but interest in instrumental ornamentation has gradually
dropped off.

Vocality, meaning an endlessly varied change of timbre,
is but one of the components of what I have called formula-
technique. If one asks what the others may be, I must appeal
to the sub-title (*half an essay*), and beg off, for now at least.
I have come upon this impasse in the course of my own composing. The Gregorian psalm-tones point the way, the Tracts
and Graduals provide a convincing but inimitable paradigm —
breath-taking variations on fundamental models. And I find
hints of unsuspected vistas elsewhere, the Arabic *maqaam*
and the Indian *raga*, the variation-technique of *gamelan* music. But to deal with this matter systematically and responsi-
bly is beyond me. It cannot be done by the hints and clues
one finds in passing.

I can, however, point with some certainty to the different musical forms which can be developed on the basis
of formula-technique.

### III. FORMS FOR FORMULA-TECHNIQUE

#### A. Psalmody

First of all, there is psalmody – though one should not speak of it as a single form, since differently structured texts lead to a variety of musical forms. I have spoken above of the typical literary structure of the psalms, and have called it granular.[6] To repeat, it is mainly characterized by parallel distichs, now in separate lines, now in grouped and rounded-off short lines. This typical structure seems, of itself, to lead to one or another form of formula-technique, whether in Dutch, French, German, English, or Italian (to speak of those with which I am familiar).

I would make these observations about psalmodic technique:

1. The prime consideration in composing a psalmody must not be the economic factor, e.g., will it be a difficult printing job? Will not separate music for individual psalms add to costs? The decisive question is: how can the psalms best be sung?

2. This does not mean that we have to make complete psalms performable by the people. Note that, so far as is known, the psalms were not originally sung by them, but by a 'psalmist.' The people sang the refrains.[7]

3. There is no reason why all the psalms need be sung to all the melodies. That was possible in Latin psalmody; but would it have been thought so necessary if they had understood the Latin texts better? The psalms, as literature, differ widely in both nature and structure. Why should it not be quite acceptable to set them to different music?[8]

4. Given the 'granular' structure of the psalms, as
   noted above, it is obvious that their music should
   not be different from that,[9] unlike the 'through-
   composed' hymn (with completely different music
   for each stanza).

5. The poetry of the psalms is very free. They are
   not our Western 'hymns.' Every good translation
   will echo their free rhythm, and the problem is
   how to put this rhythm to music.

6. The solution is not to be found in that devised
   for the Latin psalmody, based, rightly or wrongly,
   on the equal length of all syllables — a characteristic
   not found in any modern European language.

   That solution is instructive, and deserves a brief
   look. Free rhythm controls all, and is determined
   by the accent; the rhythm coincides with the
   meter. The meter changes constantly, the length
   and number of unities is determined by the accented and unaccented syllables which follow it.
   That the unaccented syllables determine the
   length of the meter raises the question, I
   believe, whether, musically, this is the correct
   solution.

7. In the psalmody of Gelineau, the accents are
   spaced equally with the first counts of the measures, which remain constant — the unaccented
   syllables moving somewhat freely between, just
   as in the Germanic *Hebungenvers*. That being
   the case, ought we not to speak of a hymn,
   rather than of a recitative, since its free rhythm
   is, in fact, subjected to a fixed measure? I might
   add that, in practice, the free spread of the unaccented syllables seems to me impeded.

8. In the psalmody of the *Neues Psalmenbuch*
   (Christophorus Verlag, Freiburg i. Br., 1961),
   the meter is determined by the rhythm, with
   the understanding that not all syllables are of
   equal length and that the meter is constantly
   changing. In this respect, the psalmody does
   justice to the German language. But I question
   whether, to place the accent properly, it need
   invariably be the first count of a measure. There
   are so many other ways of doing so. As Solesmes
   has taught us, an accent can be brought out by
   singing it higher, or notably lower or longer,
   whether one begins with the first count or not;
   also, by the color of the sound, but especially
   by the articulation, particularly of the syllable
   preceding the accent.

9. This suggests a third possibility of allowing the
   free rhythm of the psalms to express itself, i.e.,
   the tactus being more or less stable, the rhythm
   is allowed to move freely over the bar lines, without the accent necessarily coinciding with the
   first count of the measure. This permits free use
   of the many ways of bringing out an accent.

   In this treatment, it will often be necessary to
   maintain a feeling for the meter by means of
   an accompaniment. And there will, of necessity,
   be syncopations, like those in modern music or
   in classical polyphony. Both features seem to me
   to be quite in keeping with our present day sense
   of music. Still, the verses of such a recitative will
   have to be written out, and the expense borne.

## B. Antiphonal Song, Litany, Table Prayer (or Canon)

Psalmody is used, above all, in the form of an antiphonal song. This form, usually in the so-called procession-

al songs (Introit, Offertory, and Communion) has been
described by Gelineau [10] as a triangular relationship of
choir, people, and psalmist. A group of singers (choir)
sings the *troparion* (antiphon). This ends with a (separable)
fragment intended as a refrain sung by the people. Between
repetitions of the refrain, the psalmist sings the verses of a
psalm. All is concluded by a repetition of the troparion
(choir) and the refrain (people).

In every antiphonal song, it is highly desirable to employ the formula-technique, especially in the psalm verses
and in the (possibly) alternating refrain. If each verse, and
hence each new text, is set to an independent tone, the
composer is naturally going to be led by the text. This
not only tends toward tone-painting and emotionalism, but
draws the attention, remarkably enough, to the music rather
than to the text.

Just the opposite happens when the formula-technique
is used. The text comes into its own, and because of the
double factor — the soberness of the music and the under-
lining of the text — such a song fits better into the liturgy
as a whole, its form being 'open,' in contrast to the 'closed'
form of the song (or hymn). Formula-technique excludes
all autonomy, especially when used for a recitative: who
could ever whistle *that*? [11]

The *litany* form involves the continuous repetition of
a short element. One possibility is solo-and-response. Better
still is alternate singing by the two halves of the congregation
(like the alternating psalmody of the Office and the traditional way of singing the Gloria and Credo). Both usages
presuppose the use of the formula-technique: a constant
melody with a changing text. Note, in whatever use of the
formula-technique, the text is not to be adapted to the
formula (as in the verse form of a song), but the formula
is to be adapted to the text.

This is even more true in the case of the *table prayer* or *canon.* The texts are often rather erratic in structure, and make almost impossible demands upon the formula-technique. An accent in the wrong place can change the meaning, especially in Germanic languages like Dutch. Nonetheless, as I see it, the formula-technique is the only available solution, if the people are to share in the singing.

**Notes — Chapter Five**

1. See Chapter One, p. 22, at footnote 7.

2. But it occurs, generally, as *sol—la—sol—mi.*

3. For example, singers use the 'ah' and 'ee' sounds for added resonance, instead of using their voices to say these sounds *more expressively.*

4. Jean Jeanneteau has delineated how the feel for the Latin word determined the rhythm and the modalities in classical Gregorian melodies. See his *Le chant liturgique après Vatican II* (Fleuris-Paris, 1965), p. 165, ff.

5. I propose that the unexpected lightness of a note be indicated by placing the Latin prosody sign for 'short' [⏑] above the note.

6. See B. Huijbers, "Toonzetting van de processiegezangen," *Gregoriusblad*, Vol. 90 (1966), pp. 345-365.

7. See the somewhat neglected but important work, Helmut Leeb, *Die Psalmodie bei Ambrosius* (Herder-Wien, 1967).

8. This remark is not directed against the use of psalm-models or psalm-formulas in general; on the contrary, the 'granular' structure of the psalms and the avoidance of pathetic melodies would seem to demand it. See *infra*, p. 100, f.

9. Compare p. 36.

10. J. Gelineau, "Le chante d'entrée," *Eglise qui chante*, no. 71-72, "Les chants processionaux," pp. 8-20.

11. Compare p. 32, f.

# Chapter Six

## Magic and Sacralism
## in Church Music

For nearly two centuries, liturgical scholars have been researching the evolution of the Roman liturgy, and liturgists have sought to interpret their findings for both priests and people. The aim was to enable all to experience the liturgy as well as possible.

Meanwhile, major philosophers and theologians were wrestling with the knotty question of the relationship between religion and faith, faith and reason, etc. Here we would count the work of Kant, Hegel, Schleiermacher, Kierkegaard, Barth and Bonhoeffer, Bultmann and the neo-Bultmannians. And closer to us, the death-of-God theologians, and secular theology.

Liturgical renewal, as liturgy itself, is so profoundly rooted in theological and philosophical questions and answers that we must state, briefly and simply, some of the questions which agitated this formidable array of thinkers.

— To what extent does everything which is taught, said, and done as Religion correspond to truth?

— Does the God of religion really exist?

— If so, what certainty can the human spirit achieve with respect to God, of whom we would seem to lack all empirical knowledge?

— Is there any human capacity, religious or not, other than sheer reflexive understanding, by which we may know that God exists?

— Supposing God's existence, what kind of human behavior, human response to him is possible? What kind of real contact, if any?

— Can such a response or contact ever be less problematic than he — his existence, reality?

— In light of such questions, how ought one to judge all phenomena within the domain of religion, e.g., the revelation of Yahweh to the Israelites, in Jesus, and in an institutionalized Church; the sacred Scripture, dogmas, morality?

As is evident, no serious effort to do liturgy, to renew it, restore it, preserve it or whatever, can ignore the reality of such questions, affecting its very premises. To do so would lead directly to the magic and sacralism which wither the fruit when the roots are drying up.

And, to date, these questions have not been dealt with in a way that properly respects and engages the very people for whom they are crucial — the congregation, nor have the liturgists and the theologians achieved the kind of serious professional contact both groups require if any real progress is to be made. As a practising liturgist and composer/director of Church music for many years who has read and reflected on theology, I presume to offer the modest effort at rapport in the following pages.

No doubt, liturgists and Church musicians should not
try to solve the theological problems; but the theologian's
treatment of religion, especially of liturgy, must engage the
close attention of the liturgist. I would suggest, too, that
the latter's close contact with the people of God has provided him with something essential to say to the theologian,
as well.

The vices to which liturgy (religion-as-celebration) is
prone (at least!), according to the theologians, are especially
*magic* and *sacralism*, which they see as coinciding nowadays.
I propose to detail these two problems, then to delineate
the answer made by the distinguished contemporary theologian Schillebeeckx, which I endorse, and finally I shall attempt
to apply the principles and guidance thus established to liturgical music.

## MAGIC

In this context, by *magic* I mean: a self-contained,
autonomous complexus of actions, words, and music which
attempts to influence a higher power (God) for the welfare
of those engaged in that complexus of actions, words, and
music. The criticism that liturgy is a form of magic comes
mainly from the proponents of a 'a religionless Christianity,'
and who thus doubt, indeed deny, the value of religion
itself, drawing heavily from the critique of Barth.

They deny the basic supposition of religion, that man
is capable of forming a bond, establishing contact with God,
with the world of God. There is, they concede, such a
Being and world. But, they insist, he so far transcends man
and man's world that 'contact' is impossible. He is not
accessible, and the practices of religion belie its seeming
affirmation of his transcendence. For those practices, however explained, finally suppose that man can draw God into
his own world, can influence him, and thus inevitably control him, in some measure placing him in man's power. And
this they see as the very stuff of magic.

Their objection goes beyond people's perennial effort
to make God a simple remedy for their ills and the world's
problems: war, injustice, disease, anxiety, natural calamities,
all those problems which man must solve for himself. God-
as-remedy is clearly too small a God. Their objection is to
the underlying 'medium' — call it prayer of intercession —
which purports to reach him but would, in fact, overreach
him, establish a kind of super-God or 'demon,' precisely
an element of magic. Neglect of this medium then, quite
naturally, induces anxiety that one is missing salvation,
losing his grip upon God.

Does our present liturgical practice, including our music and texts and our use of them, endow such criticism
with any validity, help to explain the origin of its concerns?
Let us look, for a moment, with the eyes of our critics, at
the complexus of usages and structures they see. Public
prayer, penance, sacrifice, rites, a mediating priesthood,
sacraments working *ex opere operato* (by their own power,
just 'flowing through' their minister), a Church with this
array at its disposal, complete with guarantees.

I deal here with a question of fact, and I assert, as a
fact, that our Church practice has long been infected with
a *ritualism* (and very largely still is) which gives very real
grounds for such criticism, to say the least.

That practice has, in fact, presumed to be placing
people before God, in contact with him, standing in his
presence, through ritual-become-autonomous, uncoupled,
which is what I mean by ritual become ritualism.

Ritualism does not face and ask the honest question:
is it working? With the weight of tradition, Church law
and discipline, it imposes an order of service without an in-
formed concern about the crucial question whether it is
functional. Speaking Latin when nobody understands it.
Mouthing a formula, placing an action, which would secure

the validity of a sacrament even when neither the words
nor the deed are understood.[1]

Church music has contributed a good share to such
ritualism, and still moves in a quasi-magical aura, obscuring
very often the plain fact that 'contact' with God is not just
a sense that the void between him and us is small. By seeming to fill it up, it has often seemed to close it, and has thus
functioned as an ersatz for Someone who is not there. Too
easily, we have supposed that singing our words, whether the
Gospel, the Our Father, acclamations, or blessings, 'elevates'
them in such a way as to put us in contact with God. Music, like all things, has at times served as idol.

Here I would include:  holding immovably to a fixed
order of songs or to a stereotyped performance of an Ordinary; use of a meaningless Proper, vernacular and all. And
from a past whose influence is largely still with us in new
guise:  the invariable special tonality of the sung *et incarnatus
est* and, to a lesser extent, the *Qui tollis*; the prescribed
singing of the *Pater Noster*, no matter how abysmal and
excruciating for both celebrant and auditors!  The list is
incredibly long, moreover:  the exclusion of women from
the choir, no matter how well they sang, in favor of a
boys' choir, no matter how poor; the federal case made of
whether women may read publicly in Church, or their
daughters present the cruets, etc., as full-fledged Servers.
Indeed, the whole amazing phenomenon of a so-called *jus
musicae liturgicae* (Law for Liturgical Music) seems to me,
in fact, ritualistic, however well intended.

Consider the historical functioning of the choir, nearly
a case history of rampant ritualism.  The liturgy we have in-
herited grew to maturity, as we have seen, in monasteries
and cathedrals.  'Choir song' was supposed to be the song
sung by the people.  But this is true ritual talk; it was sung
by the monks and the canons, while the people listened.
So much for folk song.  'People' had come to mean the
people of the cloister, i.e., monks.  Lacking them, a corps

of specialists, paid and unpaid, were mustered for duty. This new non-monk elite filled the breach with their quite specific ritual song.

They preserved the ritual name, choir, and until the 17th century the whole of choir literature was composed for them, its custodians. This arrangement entailed, please note, another liturgical function as complement — listening to the choir. Thus, fatefully, the entire musical development was oriented toward being listened to, rather than toward being performed. For genuine liturgical reasons or musical reasons? No. For ritual reasons grown ritualistic. And the music it has bequeathed us, the church music repertoire, is a musical expression of this liturgically impossible situation.

If the choir, being composed, after all, of people, betrayed their origins here and there, lapsed toward folk song or stirred themselves in the new polyphony, the authorities acted to save them. And to save the 'clarity' of the Latin texts (clear to whom?) and the 'sacred' character of the ecclesial atmosphere.

### SACRALISM

The objection that religion (and hence its liturgy) has been mired in the vice of *sacralism*, i.e., that it is too sacral, too 'holy,' comes from the so-called secular theologians. Their objection seems, at first glance, quite different from the preceding one. Its proponents do not object to the notion of 'contact with God' but to the idea that such contact is to be made by a high reach, out of this world, into the clime of the 'supernatural,' the sacral. They insist: if God exists, he must exist in the continuum and depths of this world. It is here that he is to be found. Seeking him elsewhere is just a way to avoid our real task, the building of the Kingdom here, with all its problems — social, economic, political, interpersonal. It becomes, indeed, the Marxian opiate.

The secular theologians reproach the religious man
with being too little engaged with this world, under the
aegis of a Church which has consistently opposed science
and human development (abstaining, overtly, from 'politics'). And it would see the strangeness of liturgy (including
its ancient Hebraic and scriptural language and flavor) as
breeding and reinforcing man's alienation, from neighbor,
world, and therefore from God. Sacraments, the 'supernatural,' 'indelible character,' moral absolutes insensitive
to new knowledge and situations – all are seen as in need
of demythologization.

These and other powerful currents in the general
culture are surely, somehow, "signs of the times." They
need careful reading, to be sure. But to ignore them is
to seek in vain for a living religion and liturgy. They deeply
affect the daily lives of our people, and hence, their belief
and liturgical celebration, in both form *and content*. No
single discipline can deal with the problems they address.
I plead, again, for an interdisciplinary and holistic approach.

The questions implied in secular theology for church
music are, I think, fairly evident and valuable. They caution against songs and music which would lead us out of
this world when we come to seek contact with God, isolate
us from each other by *idolizing* God. The heart of the
criticism touches upon all that characterizes church music:
slow and rhythmless singing, obsessive avoidance of anything suggesting the dance, a consecrated and increasingly
inoperative kind of language, all the archaism employed to
convey the strangeness of God. Here, too, I would place
the use to which we have put the 'old' styles – of Gregorian, classical polyphony, J. S. Bach. Once quite ordinary
and contemporary, they have been invested with the hazy
aura of the past, nostalgia aspiring to be mystical. Sacralistic,
too, has been the intolerant preference for certain instruments,
especially the organ, while other instruments have been allowed only grudgingly – and, with the exception of the
guitar, those used for popular music not at all.

## MAGIC AND SACRALISM: PARTNERS

The two charges made against religion and liturgy seem, as noted earlier, to be mutually exclusive: God is drawn too much into our world, for our advantage — no — God is sought too much beyond our world, to our disadvantage. But these two charges join forces, really, in contemporary theological literature. As is fitting, since they are really partners. They are joined by their mutual involvement with 'strangeness': magic needs strangeness, and sacralism supplies it; but sacralism thrives, in turn, on the very strangeness required by magic. A version, perhaps, of supply and demand.

This interplay may be observed in the curious history of the rhythm of Gregorian melodies. What took place? How did sacralism both express and nourish magic?

Since the 10th century every trace of the original rhythm was lost, causing Gregorian itself to become known as *cantus planus*, plain chant. But note, even the most minute rhythmical marks were carefully copied, long after anyone knew what they meant or how to execute them. And every note of the melodies was religiously preserved, though in a way that flatly contradicted the nature of the music.

How explain this? Did they still like the music, in spite of its unsatisfying performance? No. Because it belonged to the mysterious (strange, anyhow) and sacred inheritance called Gregorian Chant, to be preserved at any cost within the equally mysterious and sacred Roman liturgy. Beyond any doubt, Gregorian chant had come to symbolize the other world, as surely as that dove depicted on Pope Gregory's shoulder, chirping the notes into his ear, the Holy Spirit of the sacred book of music!

This attitude, moreover, pervaded Latin church music and Latin liturgy. Both were strange to the people, and they reinforced each other on the strength of their common strangeness. Could estrangement be far off?

So it was: a liturgy which was strange, unfamiliar, unpopular, with a music to match, did not exactly 'have them in the aisles.' Increasingly, in fact, it did not even have them in the pews. Measures were taken. The Council of Trent imposed attendance at mass on Sundays and stated Holy Days *under pain of grave sin*, unless prevented by reasonable cause. This situation contrasted tellingly with the generally good attendance at the so-called Devotions.

Thus, liturgy and church music made each other's existence possible, before a mostly silent weekly audience who could absent themselves only at peril to their eternal salvation, the definitive loss of that other world. And they had come to need that world very much, indeed. The strange liturgy, language, dress, gestures, and music came to them from out the strange other world, spoke and sang of it, evoked it, conjured it, played upon something in the human psyche that likes to dream utopias (sacralism), to make mystery of unintelligible words and prescribed routines for salvation (magic). In that liturgy-with-music, a true symbiosis, music was full partner.

I would not so much beat the dead horse as perform a promising autopsy. The Latin repertoire died with the Latin liturgy. Henceforth, liturgy and church music must speak of this world, in a truly intelligible vernacular, in the music of the people. And it will have to deal with its own theological roots and needs, and attempt to reconcile itself with the criticisms from contemporary and recent theologians outlined above, in some kind of reasoned and reasonable perspective.

**LITURGICAL PERSPECTIVE**

The first and indispensable ground from which to
gain perspective on liturgy is, of course, its primary source,
theology. In the following pages, I wish to cite, at some
length, the theological survey and interpretation of Schillebeeckx, bearing upon those searching questions and resounding criticisms of both religion and liturgy that I have
outlined thus far in this chapter.[2]  I judge it one of the
best statements and critiques that have been made. I
have summarized his thought, often in his own words,
and have added remarks of my own.

1. Criticism of the traditional way of speaking about
God finds its origin in a modern, scientific, and inner-worldly
approach to things and to human existence. The theologian
can regard the process of secularization as a switch from a
vertical to a horizontal way of understanding the world. This
switch originated in the 13th century theory of natural law
*(lex naturae)* and in the 16th century theory of pure nature
*(natura pura).* Still more decisive were the views of the
Protestant Reformation and the Enlightenment, which excluded God from the domain of man's direct perception
and knowledge. Through secularization in this manner, the
human task of an all-inclusive development was deprived of
an orientation towards a final and definitive goal. All this
led to the current attempts to arrive at a radical reinterpre-
tation of religion and Christianity – the so-called 'death of
God' theology and 'Christian atheism,' both of which plead
for a radical Christian effort for the good of humanity, accompanied by silence about God.

2. One should, however, make a distinction between
secularization as a socio-cultural historical process, on the
one hand, and the theological atheistic interpretation of this
phenomenon, on the other. The atheistic interpretation is
not a necessary consequence, i.e., it is possible to build
secularization into a Christian interpretation and understanding of reality. We are looking for a way of speaking

about God which does justice to the social factors which lie at the base of man's religious experience.

3. However, since God, as absolute reality (by definition), totally eludes direct experience, a humanly meaningful belief in God within the horizon of rational understanding is possible only if *our human reality itself contains a direct reference to God*, who then is experienced along with it.

In the first place, you must look for those real experiences which set you thinking about the ground of your existence and make you ask about the presuppositions of what you are doing with your life. We should make sense out of the fact that so many people do, in fact, trust in life, without fully knowing the source or reason for that trust – even in those moments when they are compelled to face the absurd.

This basic trust that the future is meaningful rests on a tacit assumption that, despite everything, it is possible to be a human being. This trust can be found, in a veiled form, even in philosophers who maintain that life is absurd, e.g., Camus. We should ponder the implications of the fact that so many people, believers or not, give witness to their conviction that human life is, at base, meaningful. Such people, in spite of everything, especially themselves, refuse to believe that evil, not good, shall have the last word. Does not this situation, often existing before a person has even raised the religious question, already involve a decision for or against God? As a believer myself, I must indeed interpret it as follows: everyone accepts or denies, long before explicitly posing the religious question, that factual human existence is *a promise of salvation* that cannot be explained from concrete human existence itself.

4. This interpretation contains a fundamental criticism of the closed secular character of the 'Christian atheism' of radical theology (which excludes whatever liturgy, obviously), but at the same time it still shows a proper appreciation for

one of its most profound suggestions.  For it is now clear
that one can hardly maintain that a reflexive 'natural knowledge of God' is indispensible for understanding Christianity.
Indeed, an understandable, appealing, and explicit Christianity rests today upon a different pre-understanding and pre-
experience, namely, radical engagement in the world out of
concern for our fellow human beings, and resistance to
every form of evil and injustice.

5. Engagement in the inner-worldly, experienced as
*religion*, belongs, therefore, to the very essence of the
Christian faith.  But — and this will be the vital amplification —
God's gift is realized in history *in and through our believing,
active trust.*  On the one hand, one can say that the Church,
as a community of the faithful:  (1) is a point of contact
for God's action in this world through its active hope; (2)
articulates this action of God, i.e., gives it a name, as witness
for the whole world; (3) proclaims the unconscious hope of
the world; and (4) must place itself in the front ranks for
humanizing the world, must be avant-garde because of its
concern for humanity.  (In four points, what better summary
of the content of liturgical renewal?)

But, on the other hand, one must say that the Church
cannot carry out this mission and function unless it has an
ecclesiastical life of its own which nourishes these functions.
In other words, unless it celebrates, in thankful acknowledge-
ment, that reality out of which the world can live:  Jesus
Christ, the Lord, the absolute and gratuitous presence of
the living God.  Belief in God essentially implies intersub-
jectivity, being aware in faith of an absolute, personal
*Gegenüber* or 'counterpart,' through whom dialogue with
God becomes possible.  In religion we are dealing with
Someone, not merely with humanity and its history.  And
this is precisely what is visibly expressed and proclaimed
in the Church's liturgy of word and sacrament.

If the Church has no message of its own, no promise
which the world itself cannot articulate for us, then it has

indeed no further reason for existence. Only a Church
which shows a face of its own and gives a name of its own
to secular concern for our fellow man, and which can ex-
pose, proclaim, and festively commemorate the personal,
definitive meaning of this concern – only such a Church
still has something to say to a secularized world, and it is
precisely then that it has its most beautiful opportunities
for life in a secular world. If God is not an infra-personal
being, a vague 'underpinning' or mystic-cosmic-primeval
ground of our existence, but a living God – and that is still,
after all demythologizing, the core of biblical revelation –
then Christianity implies also explicit attention to the personal *Gegenüber*, an attention moreover which we can bring
to expression in a viable manner only in earthly shapes.

 6. In this respect, the praying man (and the singing
man) will never succeed in directing his attention to God
purely and simply. The divine nearness manifests itself
only, as mystics correctly say, in *l'expérience d'un mur*
(the experience of a wall). Praying (and singing), the believer runs into a blind wall, and whoever experiences it
otherwise may speak with as much fire as he pleases about
the experience of prayer. One can only say of him that
he does not know what praying is, and is deceiving himself.
God is not 'separately obtainable.' The believer knows
that he is present, but experiences that presence only in
the painful realization of an 'absence,' which yet betrays
a very intimate nearness, and thus keeps hope alive. (Is
it not precisely one of the tasks of church music to evoke
that nearness of the Absent One?)

 Simply to be silent about and toward God, to 'hush
God up,' can cause a still more lethal short-circuit than
can our misformed and stunted speaking about and to God,
who simply transcends every pronouncement (and form of
address). To be silent in regard to God, to leave him undis-
cussed, present merely as a 'transcendent third' in our human
relations and our work for a better world, is a form of speaking which does not bring to expression the most important

thing in life: the source that permits us to live full of hope —
and thus declares that source irrelevant, or simply ignores it.

Actually, only the inexpressible is worth speaking
about; it gives us cause to always think anew. And the
place where the genuinely relevant, the inexpressible, can
be brought to expression should be precisely the Church.
Then she becomes, as it were, the deputized interpreter
for all mankind, the prophetess who gives a name to the
mystery by which all may and can live. This church proclamation is, then, at once a summons and an invitation to
those who seem to feel no need to give a name to their
earthly engagement with their fellow men, a name based
upon the deepest mystery and profoundest moving force
in human beings, recognized or not.

7. Thus, the Church is, in no sense, 'non-world,' yet
neither is she 'world'; she is 'sacrament of the world,' the
human community of the faithful which, in the secular
world, brings God to expression, proclaims him, thanks
him in Christ Jesus, and can say openly in the name of
all mankind: "God is my song." And this is, then, precisely the first humanizing task of the Church: in cele-
brating, thanking, 'commemorating,' to deal with reality.
She cannot, therefore, coincide with the prosaic, technical,
secularized world; but in it and for its sake, she sings her song.


## THE PERSPECTIVE OF LITURGICAL SONG

With the perspective provided by this lengthy but, I
believe, very helpful citation from Schillebeeckx, we may
now proceed to extend the range of its vision to liturgical
music (he has really told us a great deal about liturgical
*content*).

Music can give depth and interiority to liturgy: "to
proclaim," "to celebrate" at once suggest music and song.

Before extending our 'perspective,' I should like to digress
a moment, musing freely over the notion of 'proclaiming'
and how naturally it develops into song.

'To proclaim': to announce or cry out before/to
others (one may exclaim all alone); also, to praise or
glorify. A cry is already half song. And to find, in that
very calling out to the other, that 'our human reality
itself contains a direct reference to [Someone Else] God,'
as Schillebeeckx asserts above. Our voice, moving horizontally at first, swerves upward, perpendicularly. Toward
nothingness, a literal void, the absurd? I can only say
here: that has not been the experience of our liturgical
community. In song, above all, we have experienced the
paradoxical presence-in-the-void, from out the burning
bush which, burning, is yet not consumed, not nothing.
Something, Someone has received us – the Receiver, and
however fleeting the moment, he was friend.

To proclaim by calling out before, and to call out
before by singing. To bridge the distance, to make near
the far away, to be together there, having dared approach
the Unapproachable, upon the fragile bridge of song.

To call out to by singing means: to leave the pragmatic and purely rational behind; to open oneself and
one's personality to another, to create referents for personality, to discover that we *are* relatedness, and no one
of us is ever really 'I-and-no-one'; to project God, if you
will – why should that notion detract from his being real?
Are our voices less real because we project them? Is not
the human reality which 'contains a direct reference to
God' itself not found peculiarly in the human voice,
especially when it cries out and when its cry turns to
song?

To sing out, and then believe! To sing out –

*God of the powers,*

*come and be present!*

*Light all around us,*

*come and revive us!*[3]

To resume the question of liturgy, music, in light of the Schillebeeckx citation, I would insist that we can and must have a liturgy and liturgical music free of both magic and sacralism.

1. **No magic**, no conjuring, no attempt to pressure God, no groveling before an anonymous and elusive power or idol we make a god – hidden in impenetrable and iron-clad words and gestures (ritualism). And no prescriptions from official sources taking precedence over meaning.

   Rather: meaning, function with all the *règles d'art* pertaining to it – because proclamation, singing, singing together, building up common song and songs is, decidedly, an art, with demanding rules which one must learn and obey. In this respect, 'ritual' and church music share a kind of autonomy of function, a quality inherent in their own inner structure, as well as a need to cohere with the service as a whole.

   There is, moreover, a discernible autonomy about liturgy in general and liturgical music, in particular, as history abundantly proves, even down till today. But that autonomy must not be taken to assure 'contact with God,' much less 'power over God.' At most, I would much prefer this autonomy spoken of, rather, as a *religious technique and its rules*, and to see it always subordinate in function to the community, to the whole character and con-

tent of our coming together. Thus, it is 'de-
mythologized' or 'secularized' religious technique,
if you will, free of all magic. One of its characteristics, seemingly in all religions, is its use
of music of every kind. At times, especially
in liturgies for or by young people, I discern
what I can only call a wrong-headed and child-
ish flouting of the rules of religious technique,
simply because they are rules, and thus indis-
criminately regarded as part of the old ritualism.
But this attitude tends to produce a mindless
kind of anti-magic which makes a new fetish
of automatic opposition, one more patch of
warp in the old woof.

2. **No sacralism**:  even though God is the 'totally
   other,' he is still the personal *Gegenüber* or
   partner who respects us, leaves our own per-
   sonalities intact. Our 'own' world must come
   to expression, from its deepest level. We must
   sing on until we sing from there, from that
   humanity which to seek is somehow to create.

Neither magical nor sacralistic, the new liturgical community will not take form and find its identity in being
'supernatural,' either. From a social point of view, a cultic
community in an urbanized world would seem to be no
community at all (any more than is the city or the world).
But the basis of its gathering at all is not a flight to a different existence but the shared effort of people to experience
their common existence in a new way, not mere social exchange, but human exchange, personal engagement with the
whole of human and inner-worldly meaning. It gives the
'meaning' a Name, interprets it as promise of salvation,
gift, and responds to (or, at least, toward) the Promiser,
Giver, God of Covenant.

Music and, above all, singing – the most personal and
defenseless form of human expression – evoke and support

this shared effort to form a human cultic community that will be no cult because it is ever becoming more human, less exclusive, reaching out as well as up. It is this spirit, style, and atmosphere which promise to unite, on the basis of their humanity, that varied people: doctor, lawyer, business man, worker, parents, children. And unite as human beings, persons, at once independent and related, the terms of a relatedness to God.

Thus liturgy and liturgical music are not to effect an adaptation to some imaginary 'divine' and 'heavenly' world, but to be the emergence and expression of this concrete community, here and now, reflecting seriously (but not glumly) together. They are, indeed, varied, and there must be the most sensitive adaptation *to them*, reflected especially in the music and in evolving a recognizable language. But this must develop out of the elementally human. It may then confidently hope to reach and to unite all, however slowly and gradually.

### Notes – Chapter Six

1. Does this repudiate the traditional Church teaching that a sacrament 'works' *ex opere operato* because of our union with Christ, since a sacrament is an action of Christ? My point turns on this very 'union with Christ': what is necessary to effect and maintain it? What destroys it? Remember that it is a union between persons, even as the *opus* is a gesture between persons, from one to the other. But functionless language, meaningless gesture, thoughtless prayer, and 'godly' music combine to destroy the personal character of the union with Christ and of the meaning of the gesture, and invest them with magic. As Jesus told the Samaritan woman, "God is spirit, and whoever worships Him must worship Him in spirit and truth" (John 4:19-24).

2. E. Schillebeeckx, *Zwijgen en spreken over God in een geseculariseerde wereld,* in *Tijdschrift voor Theologie,* Vol. 7 (1967), pp. 337-358.

3. From psalm 80, "Shepherd of Israel," text by Huub Oosterhuis (revised by R. McGoldrick), in *Let My People Sing,* Vol. 1 (North American Liturgy Resources, Cincinnati, Ohio), p. 50.

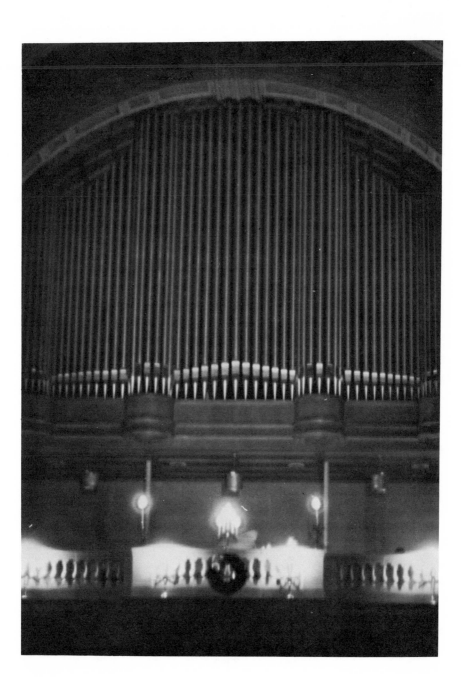

# Chapter Seven

## Ritual Music

What is ritual music? Properly speaking, it is music whose quality is determined by, and subordinated to its integration into the liturgical action.

Liturgy and its rites always imply a theology, as do (I would hope) the music and song of liturgy. When I presented a few Eucharistic Prayers at an *Universa Laus* Colloquium a few years ago (Amsterdam, 1970), a lively discussion ensued [1] about the theological content and bearing of my presentation. Before treating ritual music, as such, I would like to repeat here the principal points I made on that occasion, for reasons which will be clear from the points themselves:

1. The introduction of the vernacular languages, living languages, into the liturgy inevitably introduces a change in the musical language itself, since music, too, must strive to speak the language of the people. It can no longer speak the elite language of the Latin repertoire.

2. But the renewal does not stop there. *One cannot separate form and content*, and the change in language brings about a change in what is said. It would, in fact, contradict liturgical renewal itself, which came from no preoccupation with mere external rites but from a new mentality, theology, and a new faith. The change made in forms was not the cause but the consequence of these deeper changes, which cannot but affect content.

3. As both form and content change, the total celebration changes, including the music, which, as I wished to demonstrate at the Amsterdam meeting, plays a key role in the whole process.

4. Thus, in the case of the sung Eucharistic Prayer, the participation of the people brings them and the ministers much closer, through a style itself not specifically 'sacral,' accompanied by everyday instruments like piano, guitar, percussion. The use of texts other than official formularies can help faith to grow and deepen, free of formalism.

These observations are the background for what I would say about ritual music.

## I. CHARACTERISTICS OF RITUAL MUSIC

One might say that, from its very origins, all music is ritual music, e.g., the call, the playing with sound, the work song, the dance, incantations, overtly 'religious' music. And it could be claimed that every musical performance is ritual music, with prescribed behavior for all present, the silences, applause, bows. Think of the winner's national anthem accompanying his reception of an Olympic medal. And ritual itself may be regarded as a kind of inchoate music, issuing from the silence of inaction, with its prescribed text and timings.

Proceeding descriptively, I shall take as given that there are 'rites' and 'music,' and that there are rites with a strictly religious context.

At times, 'autonomous' music is heard in a liturgical setting; it could be done as well, perhaps better, in a concert hall. Then there is music that can accompany a rite, e.g., the breaking of bread, enhancing it but not indispensable. But, finally, there is a liturgical music that cannot exist without being integrated into the ritual action, that becomes the rite, no mere accompaniment, e.g., the Prefaces, Litanies, Alleluia. The two become convertible: the ritual action cannot exist without this music.

Ritual music, then, cannot exist unless integrated into a rite; and there are rites that cannot be performed without the use of music. Nor can such rites be prepared for by rehearsing their music, strictly speaking, since the music *is* the rite (it's as though any attempt to rehearse a marriage were to necessarily *be* a marriage!). I recall rehearsing just before the opening of an Easter Vigil, having to confine treatment of the Litanies to the barest minimum; we all felt that to go through them then, singing wholeheartedly, would somehow *be* that part of the service, that the second round could not be more than an echo. This holds, too, for the Responsorial psalm.

## II. FORMS OF RITUAL MUSIC

Ritual music occurs in many forms. First, there is music for a prescribed text whose meaning would be virtually lost without such music, for example, the Amen, the Alleluia acclamations, the Responsorial psalm, the opening or closing song. We may say, then, the less possible it is to omit a given ritual text or to recite it rather than sing it, the more its music may itself be called ritual music.

When the rite supposes a collective action, especially in dialogue form, as between sections of the congregation or congregation and minister, it is almost unthinkable that it be done without music. Such is the case with the Eucharistic prayers I have already referred to. Merely recited, by priest or even by all, they do not ring, do not communicate. The words lack cadence and rhythm; they do not act, and thus the communal action itself falls away. The rite ceases to be a rite. Thus, ritual music is verified when there is call for a collective action, provided it truly functions and has been composed to truly function.

Again, the particular form demanded at a point in the rite may, of itself, cry for music, for example, the Responsorial psalm between the prescribed readings. I would even say the psalm form itself demands to be sung. Merely recited, it comes across like a recitation of a national anthem. The same for the Litany. They demand music, ritual music.

Similarly, a particular ceremony, like a wedding or a funeral, demands expression of emotion which cannot be done adequately by the simple exchange of felicitations or condolences. The liturgy is their ideal setting, where the whole community can affirm its deep implication in these events, accepting, strengthening, singing it out from the bottom of their hearts. I would include, as deeply expressive moments calling for ritual music, the use of certain Gospel texts, e.g., "I thirst," "Why have you forsaken me?" "Crucify him!" and certain moments in the Nativity narrative. Just the hearing of these builds up feeling. Music and singing facilitate its expression, without constraint or embarassment.

Some actions, such as processions, require musical accompaniment. In general, they are awkward and unnatural in silence. People instinctively resort to making a kind of music by the rhythm of their feet. Music for such actions may be called ritual the more it underlines them, illustrates and expresses their meaning.

What about instrumental preludes, interludes, and postludes? The organ often enhances our entry into Church, as we have all experienced. But I have reservations, to say the least, about a straight organ concert composed of recessionals, music for the elevation, offertory, communion. Such fragments certainly do not achieve their full meaning outside of the framework for which they are intended. Look how well a prelude functions when it is immediately followed by its own choral composition. Lacking some significant connection, the music is not ritual music.

Finally, there are rare but conceivable occasions when the playing of the music alone is itself a rite, and the music therefore is ritual — for example, the "Last Post" at a military funeral. Or if the action be a sacred dance, e.g., then its music is surely to be considered ritual.

## III. RITE REQUIRES RITUAL MUSIC

The many forms of ritual music we have touched upon (sometimes they overlap) combine in this: the music is so intimately bound up with the rite that the rite requires the music, practically speaking, for its existence, certainly for its meaningful unfolding. Rites like these could, of course, be simply dropped for lack of music, and others not demanding music so strongly be put in their place. But only at the price of impoverishing the ritual possibilities. In theory, it should be possible to assemble a whole liturgy without music by this selectivity; in practice, it is not. Unless one would return to the decadence of centuries of low masses!

But the need for music in liturgy is not just a question of the need for it in this or that particular rite. Ritual music goes to the heart of the liturgical action because it concerns the participation of the people — and they are at that heart or else they are nowhere. The liturgies of whatever

religion, wherever in the world, should have made this simple but still neglected truth incontestably clear, not to
mention an honest reading of the continuing sharp drop
in church attendance, especially among the young. Increasingly, they do not want to gather there, marry there, be
buried there, or entrust their children to its auspices. The
dire threats and anguished pleas from high places are clearly
not working.

Nor are certain trimmings changing this tendency. The
liturgy must be, itself, an event of the people, an action of
the performing audience. It is not a lecture, a public discussion, a proxy meeting, a political convention, an organization
in session, a workshop, or a trial. Nor is it a theatre, concert,
opera, or music hall performance. It is not a decision-making
body, defends no special interests (of its own), does not
exclude opposing opinions. And it keeps no minutes.

In a strict sense, it is not useful. Nothing there satis-
fies some particular practical need of an immediate kind
("God does not help our longing. He only makes it worse" —
as my colleague, Huub Oosterhuis, has written): neither
the table, nor vestments, nor words,[2] nor gestures, nor the
breaking of bread. There is memorial, but not to celebrate
the past; reading, but the story is already well known; sharing
of bread and wine, but no one is hungry or thirsty. Thanks
are, indeed, given — but to whom is gratitude useful? And
why are they given? What is the use?

Liturgy expresses love, and person, and ultimacy, and
so cannot subserve other ends, cannot be ulterior. In principle, it surmounts pragmatic uses, and moves on the edge of
true grandeur — even while each person becomes as small as
every other. Strictly speaking, what happens there, or can
happen, is impossible. And it cannot happen without music,
gesture, feeling, throwing us back to what we really are: arms,
legs, eyes, ears, voice, song. Pity those who have unlearned
to move to music and to sing, because they have forgotten

that they have bodies; and if they be Western males, they may not adorn themselves. How shall they celebrate, if they have not even music? Rite needs music; I have seen it – and heard it.

## IV. MUSIC REQUIRES RITE

Each musical event, especially when it is truly communal, tends to become a rite, not just a detached esthetic object, alien and alienating. This impulse and tendency is, however, thwarted by the traditional concert, classical or popular, in my experience. I find them more and more wearisome, producing in me a sense of alienation I can scarcely endure. I think my experience far from special, and would like to share a brief reflection about it.

In the concert, it is usually the composer, physically present or not, who occupies the foreground. Stravinsky has said that music does not express anything; but music heard in the concert hall expresses, I think, admiration, even adoration for the composer.

But whether composers enjoy this is highly doubtful; the great ones do not, at any rate. They are not interested in themselves, but in – well, in what? The beauty of the sounds, yes, but much more. The composer creates in response to the demands of his own vision; and as he approaches greatness as a composer, that vision moves beyond, higher and deeper. Not Stravinsky but this music – that is what must be considered. But the question is: what, then, is music if it signifies nothing for man? Granted, it may have no extra-musical meanings, but has it no meaning within itself? Of course, its only real existence is in composer and audience; but within them, I submit, it has that meaning which we call 'human emotion' – so evident, e.g., in the *Sacre du Printemps* or in the Alleluia of the *Symphony of the Psalms.*

The next major focus at the concert is upon the soloist (should there be such), whose 'interpretation' of the
music will be the subject of applause, mild to wild, and
reviews, poor to raving. But the dedicated performer, though
pleased by approval, has given himself totally to that which
he interprets, has lost himself in it. He serves the composer,
but they both transcend themselves to some higher level.

But what is that level? To what, or to whom, is
their expression addressed there? Especially since the 17th
century, with the heavy emphasis on instrumental music
and the loss of the word, their expression has become its
own end, an object in itself, art for art's sake, neither for
God nor man. This autonomy has become isolation. Such
music without ties, hold, or function really does not need
us, nor do we really need it. The great bulk of it will be
quietly filed away.

And it should not be. Such interment is an injustice
to an inheritance which ought, by right, to pass into our
own cultural bloodstream; and not some waning, elitist trib-
utary, but the mainstream of our daily work and lives.

But (and here is the point I have been leading to),
what is that mainstream? Where does it take its rise and
where does it flow? What tendency in music itself expresses
our sense that, in fact, there *is* a mainstream?

I find a key, a connection, in ritual music, in its 'ties,
holds, and functions.' A name is spoken which, elsewhere,
is passed over in silence: *God*. It is not that it explains so
very much, after all. And it has been put to such uses that
I can well understand the recent call for a moratorium on
'God-talk.' But here I would invoke the deep counsel of
Oosterhuis – that we must now *do* God. And, I submit,
singing God, ritual music, especially singing him together,
is, at least, the beginning of such doing. It brings one to
an awareness, in experience, of that mainstream, and that

one is not alone in it, and that it has direction, that it moves toward Someone we call *God.* It is this fact, this experience, which ritual music expresses.

I believe such music makes explicit what is implied in all music. And good music tends to reveal, to name, at least for a given place and time, what all music draws upon for its existence, its life.

Small wonder, then, that all music lived in common becomes something of a rite, even if its object be unspoken. And small wonder if it becomes a kind of religion itself, or else a kind of self-complacent absolute, without goal or ties. In the motets of Obrecht we sense a name arising. Many namings are suggested by the music, but no one understands the word as it was meant, especially by the composer. In the concert hall it is not done as was intended, hence hangs suspended there, an answer to a question never asked.

Music calls for more, refers to something higher and deeper — what musician would deny it? It contains something mystical, above all when it makes no such pretensions. It is, in fact, liberated from its confining esthetic preoccupations when, from time to time, it becomes true ritual music. For then, it does not merely complete the liturgy; the rite completes the music, enables the music to unfold itself completely.

## V. RITES, RITUAL MUSIC:  A DANGER

Rites and ritual music serve religion (of whatever persuasion), and religion serves the existential needs of human beings. In itself, it is human. But the story of our race shows humanity to be more of a goal than an achievement, a succession of starts and stops, the human condition. Precisely to escape that condition and its inherent fatality, men search for a firm and sure prop, beyond and above themselves. In so doing, they are in danger of constant idolatry, of false gods.

They want their God to be solid, reliable, predictable. They propitiate him to that end, sacrifice their treasures, their children, themselves. They may abandon thinking for themselves, in their reverence for revelations. They obey special agents of their gods, confess their sins to them, regulate their lives religiously according to the deity's prescriptions, gleaned from sacred books or the words and lives of saints. In quest of the grail of salvation, they wage holy wars against the infidel (enemies of God).[3]

Christianity and Judaism, as practised, have been far from immune to the dehumanization all human effort is capable of undergoing. But taken in root and flower, they exhibit a built-in norm of highest human import: all men are neighbors, and love of neighbor is the standard for love of God, especially love of the neighbor in need. Love your neighbor as yourself. And love yourself. Whatever violates these norms is no true Christianity, because love of one's fellow human beings is the very touchstone of love of God.

Rites deal with things exceeding reason, with Someone beyond our grasp or understanding. It is here that the danger of the inhuman can arise. A new realm is created, of word, gesture, music beyond the ordinary, an enthusiasm reaching even to ecstasy. Or self-deception, fanaticism, magic, sacralism.

Music can be the powerful agent of transport to that other realm. In an orgy of feeling, guilt, self-laceration, it can obscure what is really happening. It can hypnotize, stylize, counterfeit true revelation, true conversion, true holiness, true liturgy. Like an opiate, it can deprive men of all critical sense, carry them away to cruelty, slavery.

Ritual music is not immune to such dangers. Witness the self-immolation of the young girl who chooses to dance her very death for her god and people, in the *Sacre du Printemps*. What is the safeguard?


## VI. OVERCOMING THE DANGER

Rite and ritual music must be measured by the basic norm, and subject to the same critique, as Christianity itself: love your neighbor as yourself. In a word: communion. Does it promote communion among all in the group, and between groups?

Do the texts, gestures, and music, in form and content, witness to, and help effect, this communion? Are they accessible, transparent, recognizably human? For the most part, can the audience perform them, because they are — in the sense explained earlier — elementary?

Texts and gestures, by nature, are meant to communicate, thus foster communion. Even when directed toward God, they should express intelligibly who we think we are, who we think the others are, who we think he is. But they should be directed toward each other, as well — even as that love we are enjoined to express to God.

In conclusion, it is precisely music and singing to and with each other, which can promote this communion, and lead to acting together. I think here of ritual dance, and how cruelly it has been excluded from our Western liturgy. We need the vision of Beethoven's Ninth, each week in our churches. And we can achieve it, if all is oriented toward our people, their common life, and toward human society in general.

**Notes – Chapter Seven**

1. See *Bulletins Universa Laus*, nos. 10, 11 (1970, 1971), and B. Huijbers, *Drei gesungene Holländische Hochgebete,* in *Musik und Altar*, Jahrgang 23, Vol. I, 1971 (Freiburg im Breisgau: Christophorus), p. 28.

2. Huub Oosterhuis, *Open Your Hearts* (Herder and Herder, New York, 1971), "The Second Language," pp. 102-112.

3. See P. L. Berger, *The Sacred Canopy* (Doubleday, New York, 1967), passim.

# *Postlude*

The whole Christian world is striving for a new self-understanding, and a new openness. Critical reappraisals are needed, but they must not indulge in fruitlessly pouring blame upon the dead, nor launching sightless missiles from a distance against the walls of Rome.

However unevenly, the preceding pages have sought primarily to assist understanding of the present impasse in liturgy and its music. If the Roman liturgy has come in for large blame, it was not for the sake of blaming but for understanding the present. After all, the Germanic tribes craved Romanization and readily underwent it.

But that history remains our biggest hurdle. It must be recalled clearly, understood, accepted as fact, before it can be built upon and changed. The new saint is always the old sinner — that's the marvel.

The need to develop a performing audience through folk music is but part of the broader need for what might be called folk faith, folk theology and morality, folk liturgy. Elitism has led us to frustration and decadence, severing us from the mass of ordinary people. This holds true, I believe, for culture in general: education, science, cooking and clothing, politics and public health, painting and poetry.

The Communists who speak on our Dutch TV in Amsterdam invariably speak 'low Dutch.' They want to be understood by the mass of ordinary people among the listeners. In the States, Archie Bunker has mastered the difficult art of communicating with a general audience. I think, too, of a student of mine who withdrew from our academic course and went to a trade school. He soon began to speak as the students there spoke. Remarking this, I asked him why. He said, "Otherwise, they'd just think I'm trying to be a smart alec, instead of a friend."

Poets have not generally written for the people, certainly not for a long time. Archie is cut off from them, from the plays, the concerts, the smart books. A wall separates him from 'culture' and participation, as the screen once stood between the monks' choir and the ordinary people. He does not see the poet and the poet does not see him, standing there, an untrained intelligence with hands and feet, a worker.

The loss, note, is mutual. The Dutch poet, with exceptions, has lost the juicy humor of the low Amsterdam dialect, its keen observation, directness, picturesqueness. He has had to write like a 'smart alec.'

He must learn to write for the Archie Bunkers, for today and tomorrow, writing them along into a future which includes all those forgotten ones: the vast majority. They need him, and he needs them.

Without this engagement in people today, the artist will but indulge romantic approval of past 'folk' achievements, such as those of Herder, Dickens, Mark Twain. It is, in the end, cultural slumming.

The Church is to be praised as well as blamed. She has a history just as ambivalent as most of us. The democratization which has reached into the arts and the liturgy is the fruit of Christian thought, no matter how strongly Christendom and Rome opposed its growth. The essence of Christianity has been resoundingly on the side of human growth, and every leap is inseparable from the kind of wrenching conflict now besetting its embodiment.

And when the body of Christians assembles for liturgy, it must perform. The Good News demands the raising of every voice in song — the only fitting response must be the collective singing of the performing audience.

**Photo Credits**

E. J. Noordhoff, p. xiii
Religious News Service, p. 11
Stichting Werkgroep voor Volkstaalliturgie, p. 85
Anne Toepker Glenn, p. 91
Daniel Onley, p. 103
Charles R. Dittmeier, p. 123
Cincinnati Symphony Orchestra, p. 133

Cover design and photograph:  Daniel Onley